A Sense of Wonder

A Sense of Wonder

The World's Best Writers on the Sacred, the Profane, and the Ordinary

BRIAN DOYLE, EDITOR

ORBIS BOOKS
Maryknoll, New York 10545
www.orbisbooks.com

ORBIS BOOKS
Maryknoll, New York 10545
www.orbisbooks.com

Fathers and Brothers
MARYKNOLL™

Founded in 1970, *Orbis* Books endeavors to publish works that enlighten the mind, nourish the spirit, and challenge the conscience. The publishing arm of the Maryknoll Fathers and Brothers, Orbis seeks to explore the global dimensions of the Christian faith and mission, to invite dialogue with diverse cultures and religious traditions, and to serve the cause of reconciliation and peace. The books published reflect the views of their authors and do not represent the official position of the Maryknoll Society. To learn more about Maryknoll and Orbis Books, please visit our website at MaryknollSociety.org.

Manufactured in the United States of America

Library of Congress Cataloging-in-Publication Data

Names: Doyle, Brian, 1956 November- editor.
Title: A sense of wonder: the world's best writers on the sacred, the profane, and the ordinary / edited by Brian Doyle.
Description: Maryknoll : Orbis Books, 2016. | Includes bibliographical references.
Identifiers: LCCN 2016011805 (print) | LCCN 2016021498 (ebook) | ISBN 9781626982086 (pbk.) | ISBN 9781608336753 (ebook)
Subjects: LCSH: Spirituality.
Classification: LCC BL624 .S468 2016 (print) | LCC BL624 (ebook) | DDC 204—dc23
LC record available at https://lccn.loc.gov/2016011805

To Father Bill Beauchamp, C.S.C.,
who must have many times gazed with amazement at
what he was publishing and paying for, but not once, never,
not a single time, tried to apply grim fingerprints or stern
disapproval. For the wry manner in which he totally, over the
course of nine years, got the magazine's urge and verve,
understood its ferocious desire to poke hearts and sing and
roar, dug its strange salt and music, and helped it leap toward
jazzing heads and souls, our most sincere and heartfelt
gratitude, and our sworn promise to not tell everyone
about the Detroit Tigers tattoo on his left shoulder.
Ever. We swear.

CONTENTS

Introduction

BRUISED WITH JOY

BRIAN DOYLE

I HAVE BEEN TYPING furiously on behalf of the University of Portland for twenty years, which is a hilarious and terrifying sentence for all sorts of reasons, but after some four thousand days on The Bluff, I find myself more absorbed than ever before. How could that be? Is this not when I should grow weary and cynical about the corporation, and shriek at the shocking price tag for the product, and note testily that you cannot even define the product, except with such ephemeral gossamer murk as *epiphany* or *awakening* or *shiver of the heart*?

And yet, try as I might, I cannot achieve a healthy skepticism. For one thing I keep meeting the kids here, the endless river of lanky gracious generous verbs who sizzle your heart every time you talk to them; if theirs are the (enormous) hands which will soon run the world, what a lovely world it will be, I keep thinking. And then there are so many cheerful nuts among the staff and faculty and alumni and donors who insist that this place matters in mysterious ways, that there is no place like it in the world, that some odd combination of passion and poetry and vigor and vision opens miraculous doors in our students, doors through which their extraordinary gifts come pouring out and the ocean of complicated grace pours in, doors that perhaps never would have been opened without their years here.

And also without fail every time I slough toward despondence a story comes and thrums on my heart until I am bruised with joy. I see a child's face when the best soccer player in America shakes her hand and asks her about her world. I see the face of a man who survived seven hells in the war as he tells me he huddled in a sandy hole thinking of his professors here, *they'd have been after me to use my foxhole time to practice my Latin*, he says, grinning. I see the face of my late friend Becky Houck, who, when I asked her how in heaven's name she could possibly stay in her office until midnight talking to frightened freshmen every night, replied, with real surprise, *Why, they're all my children, of course. Wouldn't you do that for your children?*

And I read the letter I received one day years ago from a woman never to be named. There had been an essay in this magazine, she wrote, that broke her and opened her, and she was writing to tell me about it, because I should know that a door in her heart had opened, and it would never be closed again, not ever, and this magazine and this university threw it open, and she had cried and cried, and then sat down to write this letter with a pen she found in the kitchen drawer. God had given her a son, she wrote, and her boy was blind and deaf and crippled, and he never even sat up, let alone walked, and soon he died, and her heart was so torn and shredded that she locked up his memory and hid it away, for years and years, but then this magazine came and thrummed on her heart, and she began to cry, and remembered a moment when she was bathing him, and a bar of sunlight hit his face, and he turned into the light as he felt the light caress him, and he smiled and laughed at the kiss of the light, and she had not thought of that moment in years and years, and now she would never forget it ever again.

This university did that. This university does that a thousand times a day in ways we'll never know. When I have dark days, when I have days I think the University of Portland is a muddled corporation no different than a thousand other colleges, when I have days I shriek at the cost, and snarl with fury at all the kids who should be here and can't afford it, I think of that letter. We did that. We open the most stunning doors, through which the most stunning light gets in and out. No one can count the number and nature of the doors we open. Isn't that great?

Brian Doyle is the editor of Portland Magazine *and the author most recently of the novel* Chicago.

AN ELEVATOR IN UTAH

On how children make despair look stupid.

David James Duncan

I'M DRIVING THE INTERSTATE into Ogden, April 2003. Forty years ago my Grandpa Duncan, an itinerant cowboy, died alone in this town. What would he think of the sci-fi convention it's become today? American flags fly from every car antenna, and four flags (two front, two back) fly from most of the pickups. A Dodge Ram tailgates me a while, then blasts by doing ninety, its quadruple Old Glories raggling so fiercely they'll be shreds in a week.

"More'n one way to desecrate a flag," I can't help but mutter.

When I reach my hotel I head straight for the bar—to find it's alcohol-free. Joseph Smith, you dog! Three wall-mounted televisions blare Fox News portrayals of "us" mowing down "them" while the Coke-sipping patrons cheer as if it's football. The word *Iraqi*, I notice, is now invariably pronounced the way my cracker forebears pronounced *Eye-talian.*

My wife is Eye-talian. My father is dying in a distant city the same way his father died here. I want to hold her. I want to see him. But I've come to earn a living. For the next two days my job is to represent contemporary Western American literature to the children of all the flag ragglers—kids the same age as those working the joysticks and screens that spray the blood in this war. I can think of some contemporary lit I wouldn't mind sharing. Jim Harrison: *Late in life I've lost my country. Everywhere . . . the malice of unearned power . . .*

I trudge back to the lobby and check in. My room's on the seventh floor. The elevator's doors are triumphant Mormon gold. A sad-looking contemporary Western American stands reflected in them. When I press the call button I recall a dry but inarguable little prayer: *God and karma have placed me in this situation.* I then wait so long for the elevator that I give up, embrace my karma, and lug my suitcase and heavy book-bag up the seven flights of stairs.

The room is generic, but for an indigenous *Book of Mormon.*

I cover the TV with the extra blanket from the closet.

I try the indigenous book. More sci-fi.

I shut off the light and try to aim solace at Eye-raqi children, my dying dad, my lonesome grandpa. I'd pray for our troops too, but Ogden seems to have that covered.

I sleep poorly when I sleep at all.

The one dream I remember is of boys with sticks killing banty chickens as they cower in the corner of a pen.

I wake to news of "our" Iraq "victory" blasting through the walls from TVs on two sides. For the thousandth time I hear the president's gloating drawl. For the thousandth time I feel sick. I brew the dismal little pot of pre-packaged coffee and look out the window. Flags again raggle from every truck and car.

I shower, then dress, then gather my teaching paraphernalia and set out for a long day, feeling exhausted before I've begun. Because I'm toting a stack of books and a briefcase I pass up the stairs and attempt the elevator. The call button again reminds me: God and karma have placed me in this situation. The wait once more is interminable. The contemporary Western American in the reflection again looks sad.

At last the dinger dings, the DOWN light ignites, the golden doors sigh—and some kind of dharma field opens: ten radiant-faced eight-year-old girls stand before me in matching but vari-colored dance costumes. The costumes feature leotards, polyester satin vests, a lot of pastel chiffon, and scuffed-up little athletic shoes to save the pristine ballet slippers they each hold in their hands. Their gaze is a twentyfold beam of light. My astonishment apparently shows: all ten take one look at me and burst into laughter.

"All aboard!" a robin-egg-blue one calls.

I want to, but the elevator looks full.

Seeing me hesitate, the girls squeeze so eagerly together they create room for six or seven of me. Feeling honored, I step aboard. But as soon as I'm on board, four girls turn away from me and face the back wall of the elevator.

Noticing my confusion, a spring-green-costumed girl smiles and says, "We're Amish," to which a pale-orange girl with missing teeth adds, "Here for the *Danth Conventhin!*"

"So don't worry," Spring-green continues as the doors slowly close. "They aren't facing away from you. That'd be mean. They're facing away from the *door*. That's how we show the elevator we shun it."

The shunners glance back over their shoulders to see how I take this. I nod curtly, adopt a grave expression—and turn away from the golden doors myself.

They again explode into laughter, except for one straight-faced girl in purple, who is tapping on my sleeve. I look down at her. "Yes?"

"We shun purple too," says Purple, inspiring another burst of laughter, including mine.

The elevator starts down. I'm so grateful for its slowness.

"We got to get up at four-thirty this morning!" an apricot-colored girl enthuses, "because Jedediah had to milk the cows at five," adds Purple, "because we're Amish," repeats Spring-green, "and Amish girls cook for Amish boys," explains Robin-egg blue.

"If I become Amish would you cook a little somethin' for me?" I ask.

Ten girls roll their eyes and titter at the very *idea* of me becoming Amish.

"Come on!" I protest. "I love those broad-brim hats. And those horse-drawn buggies. *Ich spreche Deutsch*, too, a little. I'll bet you girls can really cook!"

More rolled eyes and wild titters.

"I'll bet you can really dance, too."

This at least gets a few eager nods.

Ding! says the elevator, and stops.

1, says the light on the panel.

The shunners and I turn now, facing forward. In golden reflection, all eleven of us smile at each other as we await the glacially slow doors, the long hall and lobby beyond them, and the flags, malice, unearned power, Dance Convention, and students of contemporary Western American literature beyond that. I draw the deepest possible breath of what lives and thrives in this elevator. The doors then open—and pent delight pours out in a wave that, regardless of how our world may receive it, strikes me as reason enough for this or any world to exist.

I duck out and step aside so the girls can chase the delight on down the hall.

No such chase occurs. Instead, Spring-green stops squarely in front of me, peers up into my eyes, and with simple sincerity says, "Thank you for riding the elevator with us."

Stunned by this graciousness, I bow.

Next Purple stops before me. "Thanks a lot!" she says emphatically.

When I turn my back to shun her purpleness, the girls burst into laughter. When I turn back, and bow, she grins and bows in return.

Next a pale pink one, too shy to speak, curtsies. I bow. A pale red one extends a tiny hand to shake my huge one. I bow. Then Pale Orange pipes, "*Thanths!*" and Robin-egg says, "We'll cook if you'll milk!" and Apricot does a 360-degree twirl, arching so far back she's able to beam at me all the way around, and I bow and I bow and they thank and they thank until each, in her way, has rewarded the stranger for sharing a twenty-second ride in an elevator they shun.

Only then do they flush, like a covey of Kleenex-colored quail, and fly down the hall.

Because gratitude's tears look little different than sorrow's, it's a while before I follow. When I reach the lobby they're gone, but every face in their wake remains lit by their passing, and my own happiness has dug in so deep I feel it aching in my chest.

I step out into sunlight and soon-to-be-tattered flags. Clouds and birds are also flying.

In an elevator, in Utah, I rediscovered my lost country.

David James Duncan is the author of the novels The River Why *and* The Brothers K, *among other works. His novel* Sun Horse *will be published in 2017.*

ON LAUGHING
Notes on the funnest sound there is.

PATRICK MADDEN

MY DAUGHTER, THREE MONTHS OLD, is just beginning to laugh. She is not ticklish; she is not mimicking us. As far as I can tell, she is just delighted by the world. She sees a funny face, sees her brother in a giant witch's hat, sees me with my glasses on upside down, sees her mother dancing to the funky music of a commercial, and she laughs.

I have loved this kid since she was born—since before she was born, when she was only an idea—and yet I haven't known her until now. Her laughter has become a common ground for us, a mutual realization that the world is an interesting and silly place.

According to a third-century-B.C. Egyptian papyrus, "When [God] burst out laughing there was light. . . . When he burst out laughing the second time the waters were born; at the seventh burst of laughter the soul was born." Man as the height of God's laughter: that might explain a lot.

Max Beerbohm, in his essay on this theme, wonders that "of all the countless folk who have lived before our time on this planet not one is known in history or in legend as having died of laughter." But Beerbohm is wrong. Bulwer Lytton's *Tales of Miletus* speak of Calchas, a soothsayer who was told by a beggar that he would never drink of the fruit of his vineyard. Moreover, the beggar promised that if his prophecy did not come true, he would be Calchas's slave. Later, when the grapes were harvested and the wine made, Calchas celebrated by laughing so hard at the beggar's folly that he died.

The word laughter is like any other word; if you say it enough, it begins to sound strange and wondrous. Listen to the sound as it separates from meaning; feel your tongue jump away from your front teeth, the way you bite your bottom lip slightly, the quick strike of the tongue against the teeth again—ter! If you say laughter fast enough and long enough it will make you laugh.

Animals with laughter: hyenas and monkeys. Also the kookaburra, or laughing jackass, an Australian bird which makes a sound so similar to raucous laughter that early European explorers of that continent were tormented by it. There is the laughing frog (which is edible), the laughing bird (or green woodpecker), the laughing crow, the laughing thrush, the laughing dove (or African dove), the laughing goose (or white-fronted goose), the laughing gull, the laughing falcon, the laughing owl.

Democritus (460–357 B.C.), called the Laughing Philosopher, proposed that matter was not infinitely divisible, that there existed a basic unit of matter, the atom, which was indivisible. It turns out that atoms can be further broken down into protons, neutrons, and electrons, which in turn consist of quarks, which name comes from the James Joyce novel *Finnegans Wake*, because Murray Gell-Mann, originator of quark theory, loved the line Three quarks for Muster Mark! This makes me laugh.

In English, laughter as dialogue is often portrayed as ha ha ha. Santa Claus's laugh is ho ho ho. The Green Giant's laugh is also ho ho ho. Children are said to laugh he he he. The laughter of connivers and old men is heh heh heh. In Spanish laughter is ja ja ja, jo jo jo, ji ji ji, and je je je. The same holds true for laughs in Romanian, French, Japanese, and Chinese, and I'd be willing to bet it's the same in most other languages too. Always a vowel sound introduced by an h, the sound closest to breathing, as if laughter were as basic as respiration.

Some synonyms for laughter: cackle, chuckle, chortle, giggle, guffaw, snicker, snigger, titter, twitter. Just listing these words makes my children laugh.

Many things are laughable only later, after everything has turned out fine and we can reflect on our good fortune or our dumb luck. Such as my son's many trips to the emergency room for foreign objects in his nose: raisins, rubber, paper, a toy snake's tail. "See," I once overheard a nurse telling her coworker when she saw my son, "I told you it would be him."

Laughter heals; it can change the flavor of tears. When our cat died after nineteen years with us, my family was stricken with grief. The cat was put to sleep at the vet's office. My brothers and I prepared to bury the cat. The former cat was in a plastic bag inside a cooler. We dug a hole near the woods where the cat loved to hunt rabbits. Everyone was crying. When we diggers rested for a moment, my father prepared to deposit the cat in the hole. But we weren't done, the hole was too shallow, and my brother shouted, *Wait! Don't let the cat out of the bag!*

On a train one afternoon, Fourth of July, hot, tired, my son can't sit still. He can never sit still, but he is extra-can't-sit-still today. He jumps, hangs, clambers, throws his grandfather's hat, drops his crackers, chatters. I plead with him to be still as he wriggles and twists. He laughs, thinking I am trying to tickle him. The woman behind ducks to where he can't see her. He steps on my leg to peer over the edge of the seat. She jumps up and whispers, "Boo!" He falls limp to the seat below, convulsing with laughter. She does it again. He does it again. She does it again. He does it again. His baby sister stares intently at her brother. Her eyes radiate something I want to call admiration. Each time he falls to the seat beside her, she laughs heartily, uncontrollably. Pretty soon the whole train carriage is laughing. My daughter's laughter is so bright and clear and pure and unselfconscious that I suddenly understand why a cool mountain brook might be said to laugh.

And God said unto Abraham, says the Book of Genesis, as for [Sarah] thy wife . . . I will bless her, and give thee a son also of her: yea, I will bless her, and she shall be a mother of nations; kings of people shall be of her. Then Abraham fell upon his face, and laughed.

The next passage in Genesis, you remember, is Sarah also laughing at the prospect of bearing a child at her age (supposedly ninety). Lesson: God has a sense of humor, a special kind of love. God also chooses the name of their son: Isaac, which means he laugheth.

We laugh at, with, about, clowns, jokes, funny faces, children, ourselves, contortions, misfortunes, wordplay, irony, other laughs, others' joy, good fortune, madness, sickness, health, debilitation, recovery, things we can't change, things we can change, sports, games, circuses, animals, drunkenness, sobriety, sex, celibacy, errors, equivocations, mistakes, blunders, bloopers, boners, double meanings.

The late Norman Cousins, then editor of the *Saturday Review*, when stricken with ankylosing spondylitis, treated himself with Marx Brothers movies. He recovered almost completely. Doctors were not sure why. Cancer and heart patients at Loma Linda University's medical center today are treated with episodes of *I Love Lucy* and *The Honeymooners*. Laughter apparently increases levels of disease-fighting T cells, the very cells killed off by AIDS. Doctors are not sure why.

Among those whom I like, said the great poet W. H. Auden, I can find no common denominator, but among those whom I love, I can; all of them make me laugh.

That laughter is sweetest which is unexpected, which takes one unawares. "To that laughter," says Max Beerbohm, "nothing is more propitious than an occasion that demands gravity. To have good reason for not laughing is one of the surest aids." In church, then, in a foreign land, in a foreign language, one might reach such heights of laughter as to lose entirely any semblance of reverence.

A hot Sunday morning in Carrasco, the rich neighborhood of Montevideo, Uruguay. I am one of two gringos among nearly a hundred Uruguayans. The chapel is filled with families in summer dresses and breezy shirts. After a solemn hymn a member of the congregation approaches the podium to say an opening prayer. "Our kind and gracious Heavenly Father," he begins, and I bow my head, close my eyes, try to keep my mind from wandering as I listen to his prayer. Slowly I become aware of a muffled, tinny music in the air. Appalled, I open my eyes and slyly look around me to find the blasphemer with headphones. All other heads are bowed, none with headphones. I close my eyes and try to focus again, but by now the music is clearer; it's the egregiously awful song "Easy Lover," by Phil Collins. I finally realize that the speakers in the chapel ceiling are channeling the music along with the prayer.

I slide down the bench away from my friend, so as not to laugh, and I fold over in airplane-emergency-landing position, biting my tongue so as not to laugh, when I feel the pew start to rumble and shake with my friend's silent convulsions. With that the dam bursts, and no amount of biting our tongues and holding our noses shut can stop the laughter. The tears roll down our faces, we snort copiously. Finally the prayer ends, and as the members of the congregation lift their heads and open their eyes, every face turns toward us, on every face dismay.

As I write, I can hear my daughter's laughter behind me. She is lying in bed, sucking on her whole hand, eyes bright with the morning sun through the window, and she is laughing. It is not clear to me what she is laughing about, but laughter is beautiful. I listen closely, I watch her, and I start to laugh too. Amen.

Patrick Madden is a professor of writing at Brigham Young University and the author of two collections of essays, Quofidiana *and* Sublime Physick.

DO YOU THINK
THERE IS ANYTHING NOT ATTACHED
BY ITS UNBREAKABLE CORD
TO EVERYTHING ELSE?

Mary Oliver

WHAT A LIFE IS OURS! Doesn't anybody in the world anymore want to get up in the middle of the night and sing?

In the beginning I was so young and such a stranger to myself I hardly existed. I had to go out in the world and see it and hear it and react to it before I knew at all who I was, what I was, and what I wanted to be. Wordsworth studied himself and found the subject astonishing.

I walk, all day, across the heaven-verging field.

And whoever thinks these are worthy words I am writing down is kind. Writing is neither vibrant life nor docile artifact but a text that would put all its money on the hope of suggestion. *Come with me into the field of sunflowers* is a better line than anything you will find here, and the sunflowers themselves far more wonderful than any words about them.

I walked, all one spring day, upstream, sometimes in the midst of ripples, sometimes along the shore. My company was violets, Dutchman's-breeches, spring beauties, trilliums, blood-root, ferns rising so curled one could feel the upward push of the delicate hairs upon their bodies. My parents were downstream, not far away, then farther away, because

I was walking the wrong way, upstream instead of downstream. Finally I was advertised on the hotline of help, and yet there I was, slopping along happily in the stream's coolness. So maybe it was the right way after all. If this was lost, let us all be lost always. The beech leaves were just slipping their copper coats; pale green and quivering they arrived into the year. My heart opened, and opened again. The water pushed against my effort, then its glassy permission to step ahead touched my ankles. The sense of going towards the source. I do not think that I ever, in fact, returned home.

Do you think there is anything not attached by its unbreakable cord to everything else? Plant your peas and corn in the field when the moon is full, or risk failure. This has been understood since planting began. The attention of the seed to the draw of the moon is, I suppose, measurable, like the tilt of the planet. Or, maybe not—maybe you have to add some immeasurable ingredient made of the hour, the singular field, the hand of the sower.

It lives in my imagination strongly that the black oak is pleased to be a black oak. I mean of all them, but in particular one tree that is as shapely as a flower, that I have often hugged and put my lips to. Maybe it is a hundred years old. And who knows what it dreamed of in the first springs of its life, escaping the cottontail's teeth and everything dangerous else? Who knows when supreme patience took hold, and the wind's wandering among its leaves was enough of motion, of travel?

Little by little I waded from the region of coltsfoot to the spring beauties. From there to the trilliums. From there to the bloodroot. Then the dark ferns. Then the wild music of the water thrush.

When the chesty, fierce-haired bear becomes sick he travels the mountainsides and the fields, searching for the certain grasses, flowers, leaves, and herbs that hold within themselves the power of healing. He eats, he grows stronger. Could you, oh clever one, do this? Do you know anything about where you live, what it offers? Have you ever said, "Bear, teach me. I am a customer of death coming, and would give a pot of honey and my house on the western hills to know what you know?"

After the water thrush there was only silence.

Understand from the first this certainty: Butterflies don't write books, neither do lilies or violets. Which doesn't mean they don't know, in their own way, what they are. That they don't know that they are alive—that they don't feel, that actions upon which all consciousness sits, lightly or heavily. Humility is the prize of the leaf world. Vainglory is the bane of us, the humans.

Sometimes the desire to be lost again, as long ago, comes over me like a vapor. With growth into adulthood, responsibilities claimed me, so many heavy coats. I didn't choose them, I don't fault them, but it took me time to reject them. Now in the spring I kneel, I put my face into the packets of violets, the dampness, the freshness, the sense of ever-ness. Something is wrong, I know it, if I don't keep my attention on eternity. May I be the tiniest nail in the house of the universe—tiny but useful. May I stay forever in the stream. May I look down upon the wind flower and the bull thistle and the coreopsis with the greatest respect.

Teach the children. We don't matter so much, but the children do. Show them daisies and the pale hepatica. Teach them the taste of sassafras and wintergreen. The lives of the blue sailors, mallow, sunbursts, the moccasin flowers. And the frisky ones—inkberry, lamb's quarters, blueberries. And the aromatic ones—rosemary, oregano. Give them peppermint to put in their pockets as they go to school. Give them the fields and the woods and the possibility of the world salvaged from the lords of profit. Stand them in the stream, head them upstream, rejoice as they learn to love this green space they live in, its sticks and leaves and then the silent, beautiful blossoms.

Attention is the beginning of devotion.

Mary Oliver is America's best poet and the author of many books, all of them amazing.

BURYING MRS. HAMILTON

A sacrament in the snow.

FATHER LEROY CLEMENTICH, C.S.C.

I'M SITTING AT THE KITCHEN TABLE in the little rectory of Holy Rosary Church in Dillingham, Alaska, drinking a cup of tea, eating a cookie, and working, sort of, on a homily for Sunday, when the phone rings.

Is this a Catholic church? asks a woman.

Yes, ma'am.

You a Catholic priest?

Yes, ma'am.

Well, we need to bury my grandmother.

We can do that.

Her name's Margaret Hamilton.

Yes, ma'am.

Mrs. Hamilton, it turns out, has died elsewhere, but wished to be buried where she came from, Clarks Point, which is a village in western Alaska of maybe 150 people, give or take a few. There is no airport, just a short gravel strip. No big plane has ever landed or will ever land there. It'll take a few days to get Mrs. Hamilton out there.

Next day the granddaughter calls back.

You the same father I talked to yesterday?

Yes, ma'am.

Well, we got her embalmed now, so I'll bring her up with me tomorrow.

I'll be waiting at the airport, I say, and hang up, and go over to Pen-air, the local air taxi service, and say to the guys there, I need to get a lady who's deceased over to Clarks Point for burial in a day or so, can you do that?, and the dispatcher says sure, they have carried caskets in their Piper Saratogas before, so we plan that.

Next day Alaska Airlines 737 comes in with the sacred remains of

Mrs. Hamilton, and the baggage guys transfer her to the cargo hold of the Saratoga, from which they have removed four seats so the hand-made birchwood casket will fit. They have some problems getting the casket in and have to tip it some and I remind them that there's a body in there and they say sorry and find another way.

The granddaughter and I fold into the two remaining passenger seats of the Saratoga and off we go for Clarks.

When we land I see an old rusted pickup truck waiting with five young guys ready to take Mrs. Hamilton to the church of Saint Peter the Fisherman. They have problems getting her out of the plane too and they tip the casket and I remind them there's a body in there and they say sorry and find another way.

When we get to Saint Peter's they put the casket on a large wooden box near the altar. The granddaughter reminds me that native custom is that there's an hour of viewing and prayers before Mass and do I think we ought to check the body first to see what shape it's in?

Good idea, I say.

We pry up the nails holding down the cover of the casket and remove it and the granddaughter's face goes ashen because Mrs. Hamilton is seriously disheveled and rumpled from her trip. We straighten her up and fix her hair and soon people begin to come in for the viewing, one by one and then family by family.

After an hour we celebrate the Mass of Christian Burial, and after that everyone stays around telling stories about her and her kids and grandkids, and life at Clarks in the old days, fishing for kings and reds on the Nushagak and the Kvichak, and really all the stories they are telling are about how Margaret Hamilton's life meant so much to this community.

Finally when everyone is talked out Mrs. Hamilton goes back in the truck and we make our way up the hill to the cemetery, where six guys have already chipped away the tundra with shovels and spades. We use ropes to gently let Mrs. Hamilton down into the rich brown earth. We each toss a handful of dirt down on the wooden casket. Some people toss in tundra flowers as well. No one speaks for a moment and then one of the elders says there's caribou stew, grilled salmon, halibut, and blueberry pie for everyone afterwards.

Eternal rest grant unto your servant, O Lord, I say, and let perpetual light shine upon her. May her soul and all the souls of the faithful departed, through the mercy of God, rest in peace.

Amen, everybody says, and then we all walk down the hill and have caribou stew and grilled salmon and halibut and blueberry pie, and that was the end of the burying of Mrs. Hamilton.

Father LeRoy Clementich, C.S.C., served the Archdiocese of Anchorage as flying priest and essayist for many years. Among his many honors is the national Lumen Christi Award in 2005, presented for outstanding missionary work in North America.

Every War Has Two Losers
Oregon's late poet laureate
on the madness of violence.

WILLIAM STAFFORD

William Stafford wrote pretty much every day of his adult life, and while he became justifiably famous for the lean graceful poems that whirled from his pen, he also wrote reams of relentlessly honest notes about war and peace. A conscientious objector during the Second World War (which he spent in Civilian Public Service camps in Arkansas, California, Indiana, and Illinois, fighting forest fires and building roads), he lived the rest of his life writing and speaking quietly for the sanity of nonviolence against the insane maelstrom of war. His son Kim edited a collection of his dad's writings on peace and war; our thanks to Milkweed Publishers for the chance to excerpt some of Every War Has Two Losers. —Editor

TO HOLD THE VOICE DOWN and the eyes up when facing someone who antagonizes you is a slight weight—once. But in a lifetime it adds up to tons.

I belong to a small fanatical sect. We believe that current ways of carrying on world affairs are malignant. We believe that armies, and the kind of international dealings based on armed might, will be self-perpetuating to a certain point—and that that point may bring annihilation. Armies are a result of obsolete ways—just as gibbets are, and as thumb-screws are, and leper windows.

It might be that military appropriations should be increased. We need an easy, enlightened, well-paid, courteously treated army—one so good that it will cooperate in its own decline.

One must learn to waver.

The question, "Wouldn't you fight for your country?" begs the real question, which is, "What is the best way to behave here and now to serve your country?" So one answer would be, "If it was the right thing to do, I would fight for my country. Now let's talk about the right thing to do." Or, "Wouldn't you refuse to fight if asked under the wrong conditions to do so, for the sake of your country? So let's talk about *what to do* for our country."

Arrows punish a bow.

A job: To help make it possible for others to feel they can use pleasant methods to save the world. To spring off little pieces of insight and save them, out of gross events and scenes.

Can injustice one way be corrected without the interim reaction that tries to impose injustice on the other way?

What the locomotive says, the whole train does.

Does our readiness for violence and confrontation in literature have a cumulative effect on our lives?

Poetry and other arts come from acceptance of little signals that immediate experience contributes to beings who are alive and fallible, and changing. Any conscience relevant to that kind of activity will tend to be un-national, not American or foreign, or North or South, or Black or White, or East—but alive and ready to confer.

Every war has two losers.

You are rich by how far a battle is.

A speech is something you say so as to distract attention from what you do not say.

When I feel brave I know I'm afraid.

Living traditionally, the country life, we cultivate the ground. We know the seed will produce after its kind. Why then do we sow suspicion and hatred in some places? If we sow goodwill, honesty, reliability, industry, thrift, cheer, will these tend to produce those qualities in others around us? And the contrary is true too?

"Some people are idealists: they keep learning to make the world different. They should face up to the way things really are and accept them." "Well, my leg is broken—I guess I'll just like that strange angle my leg has as it lies there."

Why are there *nations* you don't like? That is a fiction you are responding to—a label put onto millions of varied individuals. Your feeling has been created by interests you might do well to analyze.

Being wrong is easy. How to be when wrong is harder.

If you like a soft answer do you have to sacrifice honesty?

"Oracle, where will I begin to be saved?"
  Here.
"When do the proofs come?"
  Now.
"Who can bring this about?"
  You.
"Is there anyone else to help?"
  No.
"What happens to people who hurt me?"
  It's cold where they live.

Winners can lose what winning was for.

If my enemies are strong and right, are they enemies?

The world and its events are out there—various, surprising, athletic in possibility—and the addicts of the fumes of belief bend over their little private glow, lost in their delusions of psychic omnipotence.

Frogs keep trying to say it right. Truth is a stutter.

Hearing the president: The question is not whether foreign nations engage in unfriendly acts. The question is why they engage in unfriendly acts toward us, and whether we can act so as to reduce the enmity. We can make enemies and then be brave: are there other ways?

You may win a war you are sorry to have started.

Some of the impulses and actions we regret result from qualities we have to possess in order to live.

Sometimes you would rather do something wrong than do nothing: you have waited for a change, and you see it won't happen, and there has to be some, sooner or later—and then maybe you can act helpfully. So—you nudge the dangerous, balanced confusion, and it falls with a clatter.

Dream: I am in an army and we are in a place like a stadium and are supposed to start fighting; but we look at each other and somehow don't quite get started. Then we realize that maybe we won't have the war. I am aware of the chancy nature of things—if we can keep from frightening each other, maybe it all won't get started.

In tunnels where they hid during bombings the Welsh would sing. No one outside could hear them. Their songs never silenced a plane. But in that rich darkness their music sounded so pure that a diamond formed in the soul.

The scar here on my cheek is 1942, a long year. It is what our country is now about. Creating the emergencies that justify emergency action.

The wars we haven't had saved many lives.

Fierce people are scared.

On a battlefield the flies don't care who wins.

Do not be surprised if things go wrong—mistakes in the past have their consequences, and what we have been does not just disappear through good intentions now. If evil could be canceled at once by a good act, it would not be very evil.

Human beings do not deserve firm opinions on certain important issues. Religion, for instance—the firmly religious believers and the firmly denying unbelievers are alike too positive. And about nations—it is notorious that nationalistic postures go with the chances of residency. Apparently "great leaders" are in the nature of things distorted in intellect so as to occupy firm positions on matters that intellectuals perceive as problematic.

Success may not mean you did right.

The public wanders from one distraction to another, carrying their emptiness within them: "I acquiesce in the deterrent of terror. I am preserved by my readiness to kill them all."

For a while, after a war, if you are stupid enough you could cheer. There isn't anything sweeter than a victory, and a good roof over your head, and a family, and being ignorant. But then your old buddies come around and say, "Let's go again, against anybody—there is always injustice." This time, though, it was different. You saw farther than the bullets went. You saw the end before it ended.

Children playing with knives. Children swearing. Children running a country.

The state can't feel. It can't have our undivided loyalty, for the sources of its power and wisdom are capricious. Meanwhile, Right wanders from person to person and sometimes has to live in the open without shelter.

Is it peace when the rockets are aimed at each other?

Nietzsche saw that the life preservers the righteous clutched were made of lead.

In every generation's picture, if you had a gap for those who died young, think of the talents death deprived us of. Our notable are just the few, not perhaps the best, but just the chance remnant.

War prunes the tree, taking the best branches.

Do I create hurt in the world? Could even my sympathy help create the appetite for it? Could people wake up to their feelings and then suffer more?

Those who follow games loved the war.

At what point does one's continued presence at a place become complicity in what happens there? Does moving to another place remove the complicity? Does survival mean complicity? Could there be a world in which silence means complicity? Or would the dying do that? Or being comfortable?

Protest poetry—could there be consensus poetry?

Several generations now have lived by values or disvalues generated by war, including the Cold War and its reliance on "deterrence" through terror. The situation continues the social qualities of confrontation, competition, power, and we now have a world balanced continually on the brink. Brinkmanship is our current unnoticed religion or prevailing myth.

Question: Do big dogs have more importance than little dogs? And people? Do loud sounds mean more than soft sounds? On the street? In music? At night? In a talk? They call some people "great" and make their monuments large. What does this show about where our allegiances turn? Why are churches tall?

Everyone is a conscientious objector to something. Are there things you wouldn't do? Well.

History is the lies people have agreed on?

Sanctuary. Sanctuary. What lives needs sanctuary.

You choose your oppressor and call it government.

The wider your knowledge the milder your opinions?

Here's how to count the people who are ready to do right: "One." "One." "One." . . .

William Stafford, poet laureate of both Oregon and the United States, was the author of 46 books of prose and poetry, among them Traveling through the Dark, *which won the 1963 National Book Award, and* Down in My Heart, *his account of his civilian service during the Second World War.*

On Not Being Good at Reading the Bible

Helen Garner

It would be absurd to pretend that I have "read the bible." Ten years ago I sat down with three translations and toiled my way through it, taking months. It was an experience of weird, laborious intensity. But you can't just read the bible once. All that this endeavor did, in the long run, was to give me a sketchy map of an enormous, madly complicated territory (a map which passing time has blurred and distorted), and to offer certain touchstones of beauty or mystery which I desperately hang on to when life leaks meaning, or which leap spontaneously to mind when I'm "surprised by joy."

Every two months the reading roster from church comes in the mail: a list set out in boxes with dates. A helpful person at the parish office has highlighted my name in pink or green. I never imagined that I would be one of the people who get up and "read the lesson." I used to think that the people who were allowed to do this had something I knew I didn't have: unshakable, worked-out faith. Well—there are people like that at our church. Or that's how they appear, from outside. One morning a woman whose husband, I'd heard, had died only a few days before got to her feet nevertheless to read her part. She held the book out flat in the air in front of her and almost shouted: "The Lord giveth and the Lord taketh away: blessed be the name of the Lord!" Her face was shining, but tears were streaming down it.

I have done a fair bit of reading in public; I can get up in most company and read without raising a sweat. But when I have to read the bible at church, my knees shake and I can hear my voice go squeaky. It's because I have to struggle to get the meaning out of the words, and the meaning is often not clear to me. I like the way the three readings in each communion service—Old Testament, Epistle, Gospel—are linked thematically. I like sermons in which these linkages are embroidered or explicated. Sometimes I take notes in the margins of the pew sheet. Often I think, "When I get home I will read these passages again and see what I can make of them." But by the time I get home the concerns of ordinary life have overwhelmed me again and I have forgotten my resolution. And anyway there is always this feeling of intellectual inadequacy: I don't know enough to read the bible. The job of it is so colossal and complicated and endless; I am already too old; whatever response I come up with will have been shown by some scholar somewhere to be feeble and ignorant—or so my thoughts run.

In the early 1980s, when I wrote theatre reviews, there were nights when I had to pinch myself to stay awake through turgid, self-important productions of the classics: my inner thighs were black and blue. But once, long before I realized I was interested in the godly business, I sat in a dark theatre while an actor put his elbows on a wooden table with a book open on it, and read—or spoke—the Gospel according to Saint Mark. I can't recall the expectations I had of this "performance": just another job, I suppose I thought, and I must have had the critic's notebook on my knee and the pencil in my hand. But Mark's Gospel was such a story— so fast and blunt and dramatic, skipping the annunciation, the birth of Jesus, starting with his baptism, rushing headlong to the Cross—that by the end I was on the edge of my seat, thrilled and trembling.

When I read in the paper, a few years back, that Rupert Murdoch was buying the publisher Collins, whose biggest seller is the New English Bible, I got hot under the collar.

"Bibles should be handed round in typescript," I said crossly. "Every hotel should have one ragged copy, and if you need it you call up the desk and they bring it to you on a tray."

"But what if more than one person calls for it?" said a passing skeptic.

"Well—then they invite all of the inquirers into a special room, where they can share it. And maybe talk about why they feel they need it. Have you got a bible?"

"Yep. A bloke I know gave me one. It's a Gideon."

"You mean it's a stolen bible? He stole a Gideon?"

"They want you to steal them. That's the whole point of 'em. Isn't it?"

I used to have an American friend who'd been a nun in a French order that started in the Sahara, the Little Sisters of Jesus of Charles de Foucault. She got leukemia, and for a variety of reasons, including the fact that whenever she left the nuns' house for a month or so her blood picture improved, she quit the order and went to live in a caravan on the banks of the Darling River. She came to Sydney one winter, when I lived in someone else's house and couldn't offer her a spare room; but somehow we managed. One morning the excitement of being in the city, plus too much coffee on top of her chemo pills, brought on an attack of enfeebling nausea. She stayed all that day under the quilt on my bed, lying silently behind me in the room, while I sat at my desk and worked. I suppose nuns have to learn how to absent themselves: I felt as if I were alone. Later, when we had set ourselves up for the night, with the French doors open on to the balcony—she with her aching bones in the bed, me with my menopausal ones on a foam strip on the floor—she read me Rilke's *Ninth Duino Elegy*. She was such a pragmatic person, I was surprised—not only that she liked the Rilke, but that she read it with such ease: beautifully, with natural feeling for the syntax, so that it made sense as it left her lips.

Look, I am living. On what? Neither childhood nor future grows any smaller. . . . Superabundant being wells up in my heart.

We lay there quietly. Then she said, "Read to me in French, Hel."

She passed me her Nouveau Testament: "It belonged to a Little Sister in Peru who died. And they gave her bible to me because they thought I was going to die too."

I opened it at random: *L'annonciation in L'evangile selon S. Luc.* ("Yes, read Luke," she said. "He's fairest to women.") *Le sixieme mois, l'ange Gabriel fut envoye par Dieu dans une ville de Galilee. . . . Salut, comblee de grace, le seigneur est avec toi. . . .*

Yes, she did die. Of course she died.

I once interviewed a young woman who had blasted her way out of the Moonies. She told me she had been so brainwashed in the sect that the mere sight of whatever the Moonies' holy book is, a single glance at the arrangement of the print on the page, at its typeface, was enough to flip her back into her state of mental servitude. Nevertheless, I venture to remark that sometimes just picking up a bible is calming. At other times, though, I only need to see its spine on the shelf to feel sick. Sick with fatigue; with ignorance, and the sullen anger of the ignorant.

I saw at somebody's house a book I coveted: Brown's *Dictionary of the Bible*, an 18th-century publication which had come down to this man through his Scottish Calvinist family. I wanted the book because it was a sort of concordance, fanatically useful, with its thin paper and mad tiny print and passion for accuracy; but the thing that drove me crazy with desire to possess it was the first entry my eye fell on: "Grass: the well-known vegetable."

At an Anglican private school one was brought up on the King James Version of the bible. You cannot beat it for grandeur, rolling periods blah blah blah— all the things people want who are reading the bible, as Auden snarkily put it, "for its prose." But a lot of the time, with the King James, you don't actually know what it means.

One day, a long time ago, I picked up J. B. Phillips's 1950s translation of the New Testament. I flipped it open snobbily and came upon a passage in one of the gospels about the arrest of Jesus in the garden of Gethsemane. What I was used to, from schooldays, was along the lines of "they smote him" or "they laid hands on him"; these King James phrases had a dull familiarity that could no longer reach me. But Phillips's text was blunter; it said something like this: "Then they took him outside and beat him." For the first time the story touched the world as I know it. I grasped that he was beaten up, like a man in a police station or a lane behind a nightclub—that he was sent sprawling, that blood came out of his mouth, that his eyes closed under swellings. At that moment the story smashed through a carapace of numbness: it hurt me.

You can't really read the bible without some sort of help. This is why I need to have at least two translations open at once: the King James, plus an edition which is cross-referenced and copiously annotated. (I like the New Jerusalem, the "Catholic" one.) Here are three versions of the same text, which I mention because once I asked my fellow Australian writer Tim Winton about praying: I said, "I want to do it but I don't know how," and he referred me to Romans 8:26:

(King James): "Likewise the Spirit also helpeth our infirmities: for we know not what we should pray for as we ought: but the Spirit itself maketh intercession for us with groanings which cannot be uttered."

(New Jerusalem): "And as well as this, the Spirit too comes to help us in our weakness, for, when we do not know how to pray properly, then the Spirit personally makes our petitions for us in groans that cannot be put into words. . . ."

(Revised Standard Version): "Like-wise the Spirit helps us in our weakness; for we do not know how to pray as we ought, but the Spirit himself intercedes for us with sighs too deep for words."

The third. No contest. Because of the phrase *with sighs too deep for words.*

Cynthia Ozick in a recent *New Yorker* quotes Vladimir Nabokov on what he demanded from translations of poetry: "copious footnotes, footnotes reaching up like skyscrapers . . . I want such footnotes and the absolutely literal sense." That's what I want. Often, though, I can't face it—the studiousness of it. I'm just too tired and impatient and lazy. I have 21st-century reading habits: I want to rip along, following the path of narrative. In great stretches of the bible it's a long way between meanwhiles. You need a different sort of reading style, and most of the time, at home by myself, I lack the discipline.

You can sit down, open the bible at Genesis chapter one, or Matthew chapter one, or anywhere you like, and start to read. Or you can scan it like a magazine. People do this! I have done it. But the thing is so immense, so complex, so infuriating, that it forces you back on yourself. If you're in the wrong frame of mind—restless, demanding, looking for a quick fix—the book will fight you. It will push hideous violence in your face, or stun you with boredom, or go stiff with familiarity—then just as you're about to give up and put on a load of washing, it will casually tell you, in Exodus, that the God of Israel, when Moses saw him, was standing on "what looked like a sapphire pavement." Or, in Judges, that when Eglun the greedy king of Moab was stabbed, "the fat closed upon the blade." Or, in Bel and the Dragon, of the Apocrypha, that the angel of the Lord took the prophet Habakkuk "by the crown" (still holding the dinner he had just cooked in Judea) "and bare him by the hair of his head, and through the vehemency of his spirit set him in Babylon," right over the lion's den where Daniel had been flung and was lying hungry. Or, in Tobit, that "the boy left with the angel, and the dog followed behind." Or, in John, that Christ came into this world so that people "might have life, and that they might have it more abundantly."

Abundance! And an answer to what Kafka calls "a longing for something greater than all that is fearful."

During the months of first reading the Old Testament I saw *Lawrence of Arabia* again. Four hours of male codes, not a single woman character, and a vast absence of psychological insight. Those desert landscapes, though; the violent tribal life of war and travel . . . Around that time, sick in bed, reading Genesis, I came on this: "Jacob on the other hand was a quiet man, staying at home among the tents." The marvelous visual flash this gives, of what their dwelling was, of how they lived. All these wanderers! Jealous, envious, lustful, cruel—lying and cheating, just like us. And Abraham, when his wife dies, has to buy a piece of land to bury her in!

I shared a house in Melbourne, back in the eighties, with a friend who had recently, as he put it, been "saved." He was, at the time, one of the most maddening people I have ever known. When confronted by life's setbacks, he used to say in a way I heard as smug, "I've got a resource in these matters." I feared he was determined to convert me. He carried a small black New Testament in his shirt pocket wherever he went, and kept the big fat bible beside him on the dining room table while we ate. I hated this. The book seemed to radiate an ominous, reproachful righteousness. I knew he would have liked to say grace, so as soon as I put the food on the table I picked up my fork and started to eat, to deny him the pleasure. Secretly I longed for grace—to hear it, say it, receive it—but I was too proud to admit to him that my heart was broken, that I was all smashed up inside. And I was damned if I would let him preach to me from his horrible black book.

In our loneliness, that year, he and I used to read aloud to each other. His mild suggestion, once, was the Acts of the Apostles. I stonewalled him, and insisted on Conrad or Henry James. Now I wish I hadn't been so dictatorial and defensive. Years later, when I was happier, I saw a movie with a scene where a couple lie in bed reading the bible aloud together, for comfort. It filled me with silent longing.

Even now there are days, as I go about my business along certain streets, when my past cruelties, my foolishnesses, my harsh egotisms hang around me like a fog—or, rather, when they haunt me like a pack of cards which offer themselves to my consciousness one by one and with a clever appropriateness, as if a tormentor's mind were actively choosing and shuffling them, so that their juxtapositions are forever fresh, always bright and with a honed, unbearable edge. Because of this I understand and treasure the bible's repeated imagery of water, of washing; and of the laying down or the handing over of burdens. I like the story of the woman at the well. First, she was a woman. She belonged to the wrong race. She had had five husbands and was living with a man she was not married to, but she was the one Jesus asked to draw water for him. She bandied words with him, but he told her about the other kind of water—the sort that never runs out—the water that he was offering.

A friend once said to me, and now I know what he meant, "Communion—I'd crawl over broken glass to get to it." It's quite simple. You examine yourself, formally, in calm and serious words, together with everyone else in the building; you acknowledge that you have, well, basically stuffed things up again; in the name of Christ you are formally forgiven; and then they say to you, formally, Come up here now, and we'll give you something to eat and drink.

Dorothy Sayers: "There is no act, no sermon, no parable in the whole Gospel that borrows its pungency from female perversity."

Well, that's a relief, anyway.

I told Tim Winton that the Holy Spirit was the only aspect of God that had any reality in my personal experience. He wrote to me: "How it works for me (which is all I can honestly go by) is that the stories work on me. That they seem true as stories, and that I believe them. Not just because I accept that their authors are reliable and their witnesses numerous and their repercussions beyond anything I know of in human history . . . but because they convince me emotionally, instinctively. As stories, as lives . . . They ring true to me. . . . Probably a matter of imagination, for what else is belief mostly built on."

Martin Buber, according to the editor of his book *The Way of Response,* in dealing with "the immense Hasidic literature, . . . disregarded its intricate theology and concentrated on the folk tales and legends where the heart speaks. . . ." Buber himself, about someone reading the scriptures, wrote: "If he is really serious, he . . . can open up to this book and let its rays strike him where they will. . . . He does not know which of its sayings and images will overwhelm him and mould him, from where the spirit will ferment and enter into him, to incorporate itself anew in his body. But he holds himself open. He does not believe anything a priori; he does not disbelieve anything a priori. He reads aloud the words written in the book in front of him; he hears the word he utters and it reaches him."

My second sister has a passionate hatred for the parable of the prodigal son. "It's so unfair! and such terrible child-rearing practice!" There's a novel in there somewhere . . . as there is in the Book of Tobit, from the Apocrypha. Ten years had passed between my reading of Tobit and my urging a Jewish friend to read it. He came back a week later pop-eyed: "Fabulous! And the way it ends with the destruction of Nineveh!"

It does?

I had recalled only a tight plot, a boy and a dog, a sad girl with a curse on her, an angel loftily explaining to people who've seen him eating that it was "appearance and no more," and a blessing the father gives to his daughter when she leaves his house: "Go in peace, my daughter. I hope to hear nothing but good of you, as long as I live." That's the blessing I've been longing for all my life, the one I have given up hope of getting from my own father. I need it. I have to have it. What's the destruction of Nineveh, compared with that tender and trusting farewell?

Helen Garner, one of Australia's finest writers, is the author of many books of fiction, journalism, and essays, among them the essay collections True Stories *and* The Feel of Steel *and* Joe Cinque's Consolation, *about the "vast ragged hole between ethics and the law." She lives in Melbourne.*

LEARNING TO LOVE
Notes on praying a river.

JOHN DANIEL

CHRISTMAS DAY CAME CLEAR and bright, and I went down to see the river after three days of rain. It was up a few feet but still its translucent green self, sliding and roiling with its complicated singleness of purpose. I sat on a rock about twenty feet from the water. I half-hoped a party of holiday rafters would float by, solitude be damned. Gradually, as my thoughts turned in a slow eddy, I became aware that I was hearing the song of a bird, had been hearing it for some time. An ongoing series of flutey trills, grace notes, serene warbles. It seemed not to repeat but to keep making itself anew. Then I realized that I could see the bird—a water ouzel, small and charcoal gray, on a flat-topped rock I had several times fished from. He was doing the quick knee bends characteristic of his kind, and with some of his dips he was turning a few degrees on the rock, as if desiring to deliver his song to the many directions. In the five minutes or so that I watched and listened, he made several complete revolutions, pouring forth silvery music all the while. Then two alarm calls—*tseet! tseet!*, like a policeman's whistle—and he was slanting off upstream across the river.

I hiked up the trail feeling a little happier. Purpose is hard to identify, and probably always complex. It's said that birds sing to attract a mate and establish territory. They might; but they might have other purposes too, or none at all. I know the ouzel had an impromptu song to sing, a beautiful song, and he piped it with all he had. It sounded celebratory, it sounded noble. I don't presume that he was singing for me, but neither do I presume he wasn't. He was singing; I heard him.

I went to the river for medicine, and found it where it found me.

The wind had kicked up. It was rushing in the treetops, whistling under the eaves, streaming and surging in long currents across the darkened meadow. *Spiritus* was on the loose. It blew, hovered, ran somewhere else and came again. From the river in its canyon to the high ridgetops, it was touching everything. I imagined it ruffling the fur of the deer where they lay in the woods, lifting the turkey's feathers in her roost, stirring the waters where steelhead held in slow pools, dark in the dark flowing river. It seemed to burnish the fierce Hunter in the southern sky. My small breath went out to meet it. There *is* a birth, and I believe in it. There is born in Bethlehem and the Rogue River Canyon, in all times and all places, a miraculous life. It belongs to none of us. All of us, all beings, belong to it.

What is it about the river that refreshes me? Many things, of course—its sounds, the cool waft of its odors, the way it admits the eye but only so far, holding back its secret life. Most of all, I think, it's the lively ease of its flow, its concerted complications, its sure continuous motion which is also a sure stillness. The river goes and goes, and here it is.

And something more. Here it is a creature of mystery, voicing rumors of distant places known to it and not to me. Baptisms, I've read, were performed originally only in flowing water, which was also called living water. No one knew where rivers came from, and yet they did know. Rivers came from the unseen, the beyond, and to touch a river's body was to touch the beginnings of things and to be made new.

But if rivers connect us to the beyond, they have also long symbolized the boundary that separates us *from* the beyond, just as surely as this swift and rocky Rogue River bars me from its far shore that stares me in the face only fifty feet away. *River of Jordan is chilly and cold, chills the body but not the soul. . . .* That particular crossing I'd like to put off as long as possible. I'm afraid, of course, but it's also that I'm so much in love with this shore, this Nature I was born to. The trouble I have with Buddhism is that I resist the notion of detachment. Why would I want to detach myself from these verdant boulders, this flowing river, this mild rain? From my wife and friends, my work? What good could be greater than this? I'm with Robert Frost when he writes, "Earth's the right place for love: I don't know where it's likely to go better." If it were given me, I would come back. If it were given me, I would never leave.

But I will have to leave, and I am some years closer to my leaving than I am to my arriving. The years slip by like an afternoon's sun. My skin is drying, my hair gone gray; I wear glasses for reading and a hundred other things. My body is enacting my non-negotiable detachment from life. So the lesson, or goal, or purpose, it seems, must be double—we're here to learn love, and we're here to give up what we love. Now and then, in a very quiet state that sometimes comes in my morning meditations, I can see that truth and watch it without fear. Now and then.

I watched the river for a long while with such thoughts, then turned my head at a slight noise—a quick *fffft*—and saw a great blue heron, freshly lit on a rock not twenty feet away. He turned his head, giving me one yellow eye, then the other. He'd been wading deep somewhere, his breast a draggled iridescence. I asked how his luck had been. He gave me a yellow eye. "Same here," I said, and the heron flexed his dark stick legs and pushed off low above the water, lighting far downstream on the other side.

I'm reminded, reading Thomas Merton, that I'm drawn to the language of Christianity. How can I not respond to those vast, resonant nouns— *name, word, love, spirit, father, son, hope, God, faith, light, darkness, peace*? To speak or write those words, even casually, is to stir depths I do not know. I'm also drawn to the activeness of Merton's Catholicism. Meditation for Merton—he calls it "inner silence"—"depends on a continual seeking, a continual crying in the night . . ."

I did cry in the night once. When my mother was dying, on a respirator in intensive care, I was strung out with anguish and one night prayed for relief. I didn't know to whom or what I was praying. Later that night, while I slept, help came. I saw my mother as she had been the day before she fell and broke her hip, only now she seemed made of light—her cheerful face, her silvery hair, her lavender skirt and orange blouse, all was radiant. With the vision came the understanding that my mother couldn't live in her body anymore, yet she would live. When I woke into my thinking mind I didn't know how she would live, how she could, but the vision was the vision, and it helped.

Since then I've felt inclined to pray. But without an emergency pressing me, I've balked at the problem of whom or what to address. The idea of a God who can hear prayer, who knows individuals and responds to them personally, has always given me trouble. My intellect balks. In fact, it seems to me that such an idea condemns the believer to neurosis or outright insanity, for how can it be squared with the facts of human and nonhuman violence and misery, the horrific deaths and torments that occur every day? How does a caring God countenance the murder of children, and how does a caring person countenance such a God?

And yet I cry in the night.

The feelings of my heart turn me toward the Spirit whose name I do not know. Whether it knows me I can't say, but at times I sense knowing all around me in this brimming silence. I sense it in the council of trees surrounding my meadow at dusk, in the swirl and slide of the green river. It's in the rank havens where bears even now are stirring toward wakefulness, in the flight of the owl and osprey, in the black-tailed deer and in the cougar that takes the deer down. It's the Spirit of beginnings and of endings, of necessity and of chance, of the one way and the many. Its name, though I do not know it, glitters in fire across the sky tonight, is spoken clearly by the whispering river, is as close as the ground I stand on and the breath that clouds and vanishes before my face. Death will loosen my grasp and darken my sight. All things are transient, from sow bugs to the stars. And only in their transience and our own, here, now, can we sometimes touch the eternal and taste its joy.

John Daniel is the author of many books, among them the memoir Looking After *and the essay collection* The Trail Home, *both of which won the Oregon Book Award. This essay is excerpted from his book* Rogue River Journal: One Winter Alone *(Shoemaker & Hoard).*

I HOLD HIS HAND

STEVE DUIN

IF YOU STEPPED FROM the freight car holding your son's hand, you joined him in the showers. That was almost automatic. The kids went to the gas chambers first. If your fingers were entwined in your daughter's, you went along for the ride. The Nazis at Auschwitz or Treblinka didn't have time to pry you apart.

The kinder guards working the railroad platforms would whisper, "Give away your baby," but what parent could heed that advice? They'd ferried the child that far. They'd kept their sons and daughters safe and reasonably well-fed in the ghetto and through the long, brutal haul of deportation.

Why would they, how could they, let go of that hand?

It is early morning, and I am keeping a wary eye on my son, Michael. We have come to the Holocaust Memorial Museum, just a block from the Washington Monument, and I don't know if he is ready for what we will see.

I'd also wanted to bring my seven-year-old daughter, Christina, but Mary Morrison, the museum's press liaison, told me she was just too young. "We don't recommend the exhibition for children under the age of eleven," she said. "But if he's mature nine-and-a-half . . ."

Michael? Mature? How do I measure that? He's not old enough to go to 7-Eleven alone on his bike. He knows the NBA better than I do, but he's not ready for Schindler's List.

Maybe I just want him with me. Four-foot-high walls guard the view of some of the worst displays—the medical experiments and the films taken of the bodies and the bulldozers when the death camps were "liberated." Maybe I trust that I can choose what Michael sees and what he doesn't.

The museum doesn't give us much time to get ready. There is no warm-up lap. When the elevator takes you up to the fourth floor—the beginning of the long, slow descent into hell—and the doors open, you are met by a huge photograph from the concentration camp at Ohrdruf, Germany.

It is April 1945, and the American soldiers have arrived. They are staring at a funeral pyre in which the burnt branches and blackened corpses are stacked like Lincoln Logs.

Dwight Eisenhower was at Orhdruf. "The things I saw beggar description," he said.

Neither do I know what to say as I turn to Michael.

"Do you know what that is?" I ask.

His hands are in his pockets, his eyes on the floor.

"Yeah," he says, and we move on. I won't know for another two hours that the image is still burning inside him.

As we follow the exhibits marking the rise of the Nazis, and the fall of the Jews, his questions come. Are the concentration camp uniforms real? Why are they burning books? How did they hang all the photographs high overhead in the Tower of Faces? Why didn't we bomb Auschwitz?

Some questions I can answer, some I can't. Maybe it's because Michael is with me, but I am pulled along by the pictures and stories of children. They stare into the cameras as if they are weapons. They are at the front of the line in Mieczyslaw Stobierski's model of Crematorium II at Auschwitz. Dr. Josef Mengele, I am told, did some of his best work on kids.

Here is a photograph of a "mentally disabled" girl at the asylum in Sonnenstein. She is nine, maybe nine-and-a-half, and she is naked. Her eyes are closed in pain; at her throat, keeping her face turned toward the camera, are the fists of the nurse whose face we cannot see.

As the Nazis developed their mass-killing machines, they tested the gas and the ovens on the handicapped. This child was gone by 1941.

As our descent continues, I sometimes lose track of my son. I am too involved to follow his retreat. Now and then, I turn and see Michael in the distance, framed in the doorway of the reconstructed Auschwitz barrack. Then he returns, seeking shelter. I feel his head against my back as, peering over the four-foot-high wall, I watch the firing squads send fresh bodies tumbling in mass graves.

Michael is in more of a hurry than I am. I suspect that he's rushing to get to the Wexner Learning Center at the exhibit's end so he can play with the computers. But when we're seated at a work station with our headphones on, I feel him wince each time I touch the screen to call up another subject.

"No photos," he begs me. "There may be photos I don't like. That's why I don't want to stay."

And we don't.

Outside, the noon sun is so bright that it hurts our eyes. The wind is sharp and cold, and Michael is fishing for lunch. Can we stop for a bag of chips? When am I going to let him ride to 7-Eleven on his bike?

Riding on the Washington subway, he asks me which goes faster, Metro or MAX back home. We talk. We argue. He leans his head against my shoulder.

I hold his hand.

Steve Duin is a columnist for The Oregonian *newspaper in Portland. This essay is drawn from his book* Father Time, *a collection of his work about children and their muddled parents and the intricate extraordinary love that binds families.*

This Soul Has Six Wings
Notes on ash and mystics and love and fire and taking it seriously.

Jessie Van Eerden

THE WAY I SEE IT, a mystic takes a peek at God and then does her best to show the rest of us what she saw. She'll use image-language, not discourse. Giving an image is the giving of gold, the biggest thing she's got. Mysticism suggests direct union, divine revelation, taking a stab at the Unknown with images, cryptic or plain, sensible or sensory. A mystic casts out for an image in whatever is at her disposal and within reach, like a practiced cook who can concoct a stew from the remaining carrots and a bruised potato, or like a musician improvising with buckets and wooden spoons. She does not circumvent; she hammers a line drive. A mystic is a kid finding kingdom in an ash heap.

The thirteenth-century Beguine mystics were women with their eyelids licked open by God, like those of monkey-faced puppies. These women seemed slipped into history, or in between histories. Though their only options were marriage or the cloister, they carved out a new option by forming quirky spiritual communities, out from under the rule of men or monastic structure. They spanned about a hundred years and covered some ground circulating a few manuscripts before they were married off or shuffled into approved orders. The lay women's movement spread like a brushfire over northern Europe. Women grouped in Beguinages, small cities within cities. Some of the larger ones, like the Beguinage of Ghent hosting a thousand women, had a church, cemetery, hospital, streets. They cropped up on the outskirts of cities in the Netherlands, Belgium, Germany. The women took no conventional vows. They were free to leave the community to marry; some brought along their children. They retained private property; they didn't beg; they did manual work for pay. They had no founder, no common rule that dictated community life. And no signing or changing your name.

Wars of the thirteenth century left a surplus of solitary women, and they also made way for a pop religion upsurge: meetings dotted the hillsides like Baptist tent revivals. Women made up the majority of the penitent, and many sought a full-time religious life, flocking to the doors of Cistercian Orders, but denied access. This huge batch of proselytes was sniffing out a way beyond a doctrine. In 1175 Lambert le Bègue, a sympathetic priest of Liège in Belgium, encouraged a group of lay women to form an independent religious community. Their main tenets were voluntary poverty and freedom. They held fast to the Eucharist and the humanity of Jesus; they were chaste and charitable and unpopular with most parish priests. They came to be known as the Beguines.

The surviving texts of the Beguine mystic deliver image-language in the form of allegory and dialogue and lyric. A Beguine named Margaret Porette wrote the controversial text *The Mirror of Simple Souls* in the French vernacular, personifying Love, the Soul, and Reason. She claimed that a human soul can be joined at the hip with God through love: This Soul, says Love, has six wings, just as the Seraphim. She no longer wishes for anything which comes by an intermediary, for that is the proper state of being of the Seraphim; there is no intermediary between their love and God's love. She taught the soul's annihilation: that the soul, in Holy Church the Greater, might have no will of her own, that it serve only as a mirror for God's image and will. Porette's book was burned publicly by the Bishop of Cambrai, but she made no concessions. In fact, she added seventeen more chapters, moved her allegory forward, spruced up her characters. She was burned at the stake in 1310.

Another main text came out of Germany: *Flowing Light of the Godhead*, by Mechthild of Magdeburg. Her first manuscript is in the low-German dialect and draws on images from courtly love, a secular tradition. Mechthild admits: I do not know how to write nor can I, unless I see with the eyes of my soul and hear with the ears of my eternal spirit and feel in all the parts of my body the power of the Holy Spirit. And, to convey the Spirit, she uses what's available, what she sees out her window, touches to her lips, knows in her body.

A mystic is unapologetic for a lack of theological education, a schol-ar's explanations. (Porette: You must let Love and Faith together be your guides to climb where Reason cannot come.) The Beguines' writ-ings play out scenes in common tropes of spiritual literature: a bride, a desert, a bed of pain. These images trigger something in me. What if I cast about for my own, for things that have caught my attention the way a fence-barb does a loose shirt? What if that's all you have? Just the images? Perhaps images leave room or make room for mystery. Image as a felt truth for the weak who need more than doctrine. You struggle for an image; it wriggles into life and is born.

Is there a place for the contemporary mystic? Can someone try again to crawl into the big shell of mystical tradition and holler and hear her small voice echo back? Can she reclaim it in some way?

The way I see it, a mystic simply believes that God visits.

A mystic stays with what's striking: out the windshield, in between the intermittent wipers, a shadow, a flash of light, color, a face. She sees something, she sees and then she runs to show and tell, or at least she practices speeches in her head. She mulls over her images, arranges her sermon in a picture book—it's like a touch-and-feel kids book, furry cloth for monkey feet, a bit of rubber ball for bear nose. She wants her images vivid.

The Beguines had two main takes on the image of the desert. Some ref-erences pointed to the wilderness where the Old Testament children of Israel wandered for forty years, in exile, in desperation, trying to make it to the Promised Land of Milk and Honey. Life is exile, according to these writings, life is the trial to be endured, the soul's desolate journey home to God. The other manifestation of the desert image is as encoun-ter: the desert isn't the thing to be endured for the goal; it is the goal; it is the landscape of union. It is, from the Book of Hosea, the place where God will allure her, bring her into the wilderness, and speak comfort to her. It's where you learn how to love.

A burned-down trailer is a desert of ash, silt, secrets. It is exposure, down to the ground, to wind to sun to rain. Brought to nothing. A melted photograph here, a charred unfastened locket there. A black-ened mirror.

A fencerow, attended by walnut and hickory trees and underbrush, separated my house from Christy Gribbles's trailer. Before the trailer burned, Christy and I made a break in the fence so she could come to my side and I could go to hers.

A grease fire on the stove started the fire. It was in late fall. My brother Luke and I were just returning from a walk. We'd seen a deer close-up, licking water from the streambed. We had been silent with it and after it quenched its thirst, it picked its way through the underbrush into the cloak of the pines. We were heading back when we saw the huge piles of black smoke stacking on top of the bare trees. The trailer seemed to burn clear to the ground in minutes. Nobody was caught inside, and they even got some of the clothes out. But Christy and her younger brother G.W. were standing outside close to the fence with smoky blank faces. They seemed exposed there to the wind and the bits of ash flaking down like dirty snow. From my front porch, I stood watching her home become nothing.

What happens, Christy, when you lose everything? I picture that charred trailer-desert in my head now, remembering how they stayed for a time up at Nolan Wilson's old place and how we gave bags of clothes and a Glow Worm that lit up when you pressed him, trying to fill their new Nothing. In the beginning, there was a home with rooms and maybe not plenty but at least something, and then there was wasteland, No-place, No-home.

What happens when you lose everything? When you slip out, down the chain-link fire escape ladder and leave all evidence of self behind in the rubbish? I think sometimes: I could throw my day, my lifework out a window. And try to earn emptiness, a trailer-desert, a sigh in the soul.

Why speak in images? In trailer fire? What's the point when they leave you winded? Well, you don't know what else to say or how else to say it, like holding the hand of someone who's lost everything. It is an inexplicable being-with, a fleshing, a new Way.

Is a mystic anyone who realizes a truth and flashes it like a strong poker hand? She is the checkout lady at the Dollar General, talking on the phone to her husband who's trying to get the title for the truck but can't, and she has to go, there are customers. And she realizes and she says, This is all too much. On her face you see clearly where her weeping goes. You remember exactly what she looks like.

A neighbor calls in early evening about the double rainbow in the sky. Another and another calls, Judy, my Aunt Kathy from town. From the porch, we can see the full arc of one, the marvelous ghost of the other. We have not lost this need to tell, to show, to point.

Sometimes you see nothing in the sky, no promises or mark of Jesus' feet, no sign that he's coming back to bring you home—so you write down the Nothing and the No-place, too.

Beguines weren't recluses. Un-cloistered, they grouped their small cabins together into their Beguinages on the outskirts of cities where they worked making lace or gardens, teaching or nursing, managing shelters for urban women and kids who worked in textiles. Their cabins made a half-circle; one could see the other's light from her stoop, could string together two tin cans, window to window. Out from this half-circle shelter, Beguine mystics attracted the urban faithful, with their penchant for heresy and the use of the vernacular, the tongue of fire making sense. They gathered in the exiled and wandering. They had a context for dealing with suffering.

I gather with a group of women in Philadelphia, all of us assembling around Jesus, perked for evangel like girls hovering around a radio. But as you hover in a circle, you brush arms with each other. Liz Lopez was a woman among us whose husband was incarcerated, and she had three boys and a tiny frame; she looked like she could blow away. And still, she beautifully braced herself under her heavy beam of a dadless series of days that bore down with the weight of her boys' birthdays, street hockey games, piss-the-bed nights. Nobody skirted around her; we entered in as best we could, catching her insides as she spilled out, ready, at any moment, to spill ourselves.

We met in Susan's house in Hunting Park. We ate and then sang a few choruses and discussed sermons. One night the sermon was on James' epistle in the New Testament: Count it all joy, he says, when you fall into various trials, knowing that the testing of your faith produces patience. We cried onto our plates of Spanish rice and chicken that Blanca had brought because the trials were various; Wendy's husband left her and the kids, another husband had cancer, Celeste and her girls lost their row house.

Often a woman takes tentative steps toward another, shy about the magnetic pull of this other's wounds. A raw, undisguised wound pulls you out of your own general okayness: your safe bed, your comfort. There is something about her uncontained and spilling-out life, a doll losing its fiber-fill, the dazed hungry look of one knocked off course. You want to zip up the back of her dresses, paint your lips with Bonnie

Bell Cranberry or Smolder, and borrow her wakefulness that came the moment she was left. You feel that you've been drawn away from your life till you missed it with a fresh homesickness, so you can see it and take off its walls and shiver, alive again, as though you've taken a dip in icy cold water.

But is it a longing for laceration? That extreme mystical asceticism or mortification of flesh and the wakefulness it affords? Or is it maudlin, sentimental, like a rhyming couplet in a sympathy card?

I don't think so. I don't think that's what it was for most of the Beguines. It's just the fact of suffering, the dealing with it, making meaning out of it, and if there is no meaning, just to share it.

Here's my image: a gathering on a porch stoop, maybe some of the women smoking, maybe some just watching the door to the neighboring convenience store, but a group surely bound to each other. The image goes as follows: a girl alone, hugging her knees on the stoop—she's missed a period, or she's lost her baby, or her husband's left, or she simply couldn't get out of bed till two in the afternoon—the fire hydrant shooting out streams in the July heat and kids galloping this way and that, and she suffers, and the others come around, from other porches. They bring Spanish rice and chicken, boiled milk for coffee. And the gathered women stay there, through the early fall, into November. They are entering winter together out there, pointing, Look: how gentle the snow.

I wonder if mystical life is really about visions, or if it's about looking again at the pieces you've already got: of a rocky marriage, a job at Dollar General, a double rainbow. And if you see the kingdom of God there if you stare long enough. I wonder if it's about holding yourself still as a mirror. Or just about making a big old scene, waving your arms wildly.

What's dangerous about a mystic?

Held suspect from the beginning for their disregard for ecclesiastical hierarchy, the unschooled Beguines fell out of favor with the clerics. The women fueled the Church's disapproval by reading biblical texts to everyday folks in their native tongue. In 1274 the Council of Lyons banned any new spiritual orders from forming; new groups had to operate within an existing, approved order. There were rumors of prostitution, sexual license. The Inquisition wasn't kind. In 1312, the Council of Vienne officially declared the Beguines heretical, accusing them of association with antinomian adherents of the Free Spirit. Their property was confiscated; many women had to marry. Many were forced to sign up with a convent.

But what's dangerous about a mystic? Hurling and wielding the best stuff she can imagine, insisting on an unmediated Way of Wakefulness. A mild heretic with dyed pink hair and a threadbare T-shirt with the slogan Take me seriously.

Today I don't suppose she fears the Inquisition and its fire—just dullness, just missing it. She fears dismissal. She wrestles, she squints the eyes of her soul. Perhaps she doesn't ditch tradition as much as take it for its word and peer inside its cavernous shell. There must still be something worth saying, worth pointing to.

Jessie Van Eerden is the author of the novels Glorybound *and* My Radio Radio.

Hep! Hep! Hep!

Cynthia Ozick

WE THOUGHT IT WAS FINISHED. The ovens are long cooled, the anti-vermin gas dissipated into purifying clouds, cleansed air, nightmarish fable. The cries of the naked, decades gone, are mute; the bullets splitting throats and breasts and skulls, the human waterfall of bodies tipping over into the wooded ravine at Babi Yar, are no more than tedious footnotes on aging paper. The deportation ledgers, with their scrupulous lists of names of the doomed, what are they now? Museum artifacts. The heaps of eyeglasses and children's shoes, the hills of human hair, lie disintegrating in their display cases, while only a little distance away the visitors' cafeteria bustles and buzzes: sandwiches, Cokes, the waiting tour buses.

We thought it was finished. In the middle of the twentieth century, and surely by the end of it, we thought it was finished, genuinely finished, the bloodlust finally slaked. We thought it was finished, that heads were hanging—the heads of the leaders and schemers on gallows, the heads of the bystanders and onlookers in shame. The Topf company, manufacturer of the ovens, went belatedly out of business, belatedly disgraced and shamed. Out of shame German publishers of Nazi materials concealed and falsified the past. Out of shame Paul de Man, lauded and eminent Yale intellectual, concealed his early Nazi lucubrations. Out of shame Mircea Eliade, lauded and eminent Chicago intellectual, concealed his membership in Romania's Nazi-linked Iron Guard. Out of shame memorials to the murdered rose up. Out of shame synagogues were rebuilt in the ruins of November 9, 1938, the night of fire and pogrom and the smashing of windows. Out of shame those who were hounded like prey and fled for their lives were invited back to their native villages and towns and cities, to be celebrated as successful escapees from the murderous houndings of their native villages and towns and cities. Shame is salubrious: it acknowledges inhumanity, it admits to complicity, it induces remorse. Naïvely, foolishly, stupidly, hopefully, a-historically, we thought that shame and remorse—world-wide shame, worldwide remorse—would endure. Naïvely, foolishly, stupidly, hopefully, a-historically, we thought that the cannibal hatred, once quenched, would not soon wake again.

It has awakened.

In "The Modern Hep! Hep! Hep!"—an 1878 essay reflecting on the condition of the Jews—George Eliot noted that it would be "difficult to find a form of bad reasoning about [Jews] which had not been heard in conversation or been admitted to the dignity of print." She was writing in a period politically not unlike our own, Disraeli ascendant in England, Jews prominent in liberal parties both in Germany and France. Yet her title points to something far deadlier than mere "bad reasoning." Hep! was the cry of the Crusaders as they swept through Europe, annihilating one Jewish community after another; it stood for *Hierosolyma est perdita* (Jerusalem is destroyed), and was taken up again by anti-Jewish rioters in Germany in 1819. In this single raging syllable, past and future met, and in her blunt bold enunciation of it, George Eliot was joining bad reasoning—i.e., canard and vilification—to its consequences: violence and murder. The Jews, she wrote, have been "regarded and treated very much as beasts hunted for their skins," and the curse on them, the charge of deicide, was counted a justification for hindering them from pursuing agriculture and handicrafts; for marking them out as execrable figures by a peculiar dress; for torturing them . . . spitting at them and pelting them; for taking it certain that they killed and ate babies, poisoned the wells, and took pains to spread the plague; for putting it to them whether they would be baptized or burned, and not failing to burn and massacre them when they were obstinate; but also for suspecting them of disliking their baptism when they had got it, and then burning them in punishment of their insincerity; finally, for hounding them by tens on tens of thousands from their homes where they had found shelter for centuries, and inflicting on them the horrors of a new exile and a new dispersion. All this to avenge the Savior of mankind, or else to compel these stiff-necked people to acknowledge a Master whose servants showed such beneficent effects of His teaching.

As an anti-Semitic yelp, Hep! is long out of fashion. In the eleventh century it was already a substitution and a metaphor: Jerusalem meant Jews, and "Jerusalem is destroyed" was, when knighthood was in flower, an incitement to pogrom. Today, the modern Hep! appears in the form of Zionism, Israel, Sharon. And the connection between vilification and the will to undermine and endanger Jewish lives is as vigorous as when the howl of Hep! was new. The French ambassador to Britain, his tongue unbuttoned in a London salon, hardly thinks to cry Hep!; instead, he speaks of "that shitty little country." European and British scholars and academicians, their Latin gone dry, will never cry Hep!; instead they call for the boycott of Israeli scholars and academicians.

Nearly all of this had precedents in the Church Luther renounced; and even the medieval Church practiced mimicry. It was Pope Innocent III who implemented the yellow badge of ignominy (Hitler was no innovator, except as to gas chambers)—yet Innocent too was innocent of originality, since he took the idea from Prince Abu-Yusef Almansur, a Moroccan Muslim ruler of the thirteenth century. Post-Enlightenment France may be known for its merciless persecution of a guiltless Dreyfus, and for the anti-Jewish rioting it set off; and, more recently, for the gendarmes who arrested and deported the Jews of Paris with a zeal equal to that of the Germans. But Paris had seen anti-Jewish mobs before—for instance, in June of 1242, when twenty-four cartloads of Talmuds were set afire in a public square. And while elsewhere in France, and all through the Rhineland, the Crusaders were busy at their massacres, across the Channel the Archbishop of Canterbury was issuing a decree designed to prevent the Jews of England from having access to food.

All this, let it be noted, preceded the barbarities of the Inquisition: the scourgings, the burnings, the confiscations, the expulsions. Any attempt to set down the record, early and late, of Christian violence against Jews can only be a kind of pointillism—an atrocity here, another there, and again another. The nineteenth-century historian Heinrich Graetz (as rationalist in temperament as Gibbon) summed up the predicament of Jews across the whole face of Europe: If Jewish history were to follow chronicles, memorial books, and martyrologies, its pages would be filled with bloodshed, it would consist of horrible exhibitions of corpses, and it would stand forth to make accusation against a doctrine which taught princes and nations to become common executioners and hangmen. For, from the thirteenth to the sixteenth centuries, the persecutions and massacres of the Jews increased with frightful rapidity and intensity, and only alternated with inhuman decrees issued by both Church and the state, the aim and purport of all of which were to humiliate the Jews, to brand them with calumny and to drive them to suicide. . . . The nations of Europe emulated one another in exercising their cruelty upon the Jews. . . . In Germany they were slain by thousands. . . . Every year martyrs fell, now in Weissenburg, Magdeburg, Arnstadt, now in Coblenz, Sinzig, Erfurt, and other places. In Sinzig all the members of the congregation were burnt alive on a Sabbath in their synagogue. There were German Christian families who boasted that they had burnt Jews, and in their pride assumed the name of Judenbrater (Jew-roaster).

And all this, let it again be noted, before the Shoah; before the Czarist pogroms and the Czarist fabrication of the "Protocols of the Elders of Zion"; before the exclusions, arrests, and gulag brutalities of the Soviet Union; before the shooting of the Soviet Yiddish writers in the basement of Moscow's Lubyanka prison; before the rise of contemporary Islamist demonization of Jews; before the eight-decades-long Arab assault on Jewish national aspiration and sovereignty; before the Palestinian cult of suicide bombing. Anti-Semitism feeds on itself from continent to continent, from Iceland to Japan: it scarcely requires living Jews. Its source is commonly taken to be the two supersessionist Scriptures that derive from Judaism—in Christianity, the Jews' cry (in the Gospel of Matthew) of "His blood be on us and on our children," the fount of the venomous deicide curse; in Islam, the unwillingness of Jews to follow Mohammed in the furtherance of a latter-day faith which accused the Hebrew Bible of distorting the biblical narratives that appear, Islam claims, more authoritatively and genuinely in the Koran.

But anti-Semitism originated in neither Christianity nor Islam. Its earliest appearance burst out in Egypt, in the fourth century B.C.E., during the reign of Ptolemy II, when Manetho, an Egyptian priest, in a polemic directed against the biblical account in Genesis and Exodus, described a people who "came from Jerusalem" as the descendants of a mob of lepers. Against the Hebrew text, which records Joseph as a wise and visionary governor, Manetho charged that Joseph defiled the shrines and statues of the gods and set fire to villages and towns. Nor did Moses liberate the Hebrews and bring them, under divine guidance, out of Egypt, from slavery to freedom. These offspring of lepers, Manetho declared, were ignominiously expelled, having savagely despoiled the country for thirteen years. Such calumnies soon infiltrated Hellenic literature. The Greeks, detecting no plastic representation of the divine order, were quick to name the Jews atheists—lazy atheists, since once in seven days they refrained from labor. The Greek scholar Mnaseas of Patara recycled an Egyptian myth (traces of it later turned up in Plutarch) which asserted that the Temple in Jerusalem harbored the golden head of an ass, the sole object of the Jews' worship. Another version had the Jews praying before an image of Moses seated on an ass while displaying a book containing laws of hatred for all humanity.

Greek enmity was most acutely encapsulated in the canard spread by Apion, whose contribution to the history of anti-Semitism is the infamously enduring blood libel. In its earliest form a Greek, captured by Jews, is taken to the Temple, fattened, and then killed; his entrails are ritually eaten in conjunction with an oath of hatred toward Greeks. Christian mythology altered Greek to Christian, usually a child, whose blood was said to be drained at Passover for the purpose of being baked into matzah. From its Christian source, the blood libel leached into Muslim societies. It surfaced most recently in a Saudi newspaper, which fantasized Muslim blood in Purim cakes. Mustafa Tlas, the Syrian defense minister, is the author of The Matzah of Zion, which presents the 1841 Damascus blood libel as an established "Jewish ritual." And in a writing contest sponsored by the Palestinian Education Ministry, the winning entry, by a tenth-grader, described a Mother's Day gift an Israeli soldier brings to his mother: "a bottle of the blood of a Palestinian child he has murdered."

Current anti-Semitism, accelerating throughout advanced and sophisticated Europe—albeit under the rubric of anti-Zionism, and masked by the deceptive lingo of human rights—purports to eschew such primitivism. After all, Nazism and Stalinism are universally condemned; anti-Judaism is seen as obscurantist medievalism; the Vatican's theology of deicide was nullified four decades ago; Lutherans, at least in America, vigorously dissociate themselves from their founder's execrations of the Jews; and whatever the vestiges of Europe's unregenerate (and often Holocaust-denying) Right may think, its vociferous Left would no more depart from deploring the Holocaust than it would be willing to be deprived of its zeal in calumniating the Jewish state. It is easy enough to shed a tear or two for the shed and slandered blood of the Jews of the past; no one will praise Torquemada, or honor Goebbels.

But to stand up for truth-telling in the present, in a mythologizing atmosphere of pervasive defamation and fabrication, is not a job for cowards.

In the time of Goebbels, the Big Lie about the Jews was mainly confined to Germany alone; much of the rest of the world saw through it with honest clarity. In our time, the Big Lie (or Big Lies, there are so many) is disseminated everywhere, and not merely by the ignorant, but with malice aforethought by the intellectual classes, the governing elites, the most prestigious elements of the press in all the capitals of Europe, and by the university professors and the diplomats.

The contemporary Big Lie, of course, concerns the Jews of Israel: they are oppressors in the style of the Nazis; they ruthlessly pursue, and perpetuate, "occupation" solely for the sake of domination and humiliation; they purposefully kill Palestinian children; their military has committed massacres; their government "violates international law"; their nationhood and their sovereignty have no legitimacy; they are intruders and usurpers inhabiting an illicit "entity," and not a people entitled as other peoples are entitled; and so on and so on. Reviving both blood libel and deicide, respectable European journals publish political cartoons showing Prime Minister Sharon devouring Palestinian babies, and Israeli soldiers bayoneting the infant Jesus.

Yet the modern history of Jews in the Holy Land overwhelmingly refutes these scurrilities. It is the Arabs, not the Jews, who have been determined to dispose of a people's right to live in peace. Is there any point now—after so many politically willed erasures of fact by Palestinian Arabs, Muslim populations in general, and a mean-spirited European intelligentsia—to recapitulate the long record of Arab hostility that has prevailed since the demise of the Ottoman Empire? The Muslim Arab claim of hegemony (through divine fiat, possessive greed, contempt for pluralism, or all three) over an entire region of the globe accounts for the hundreds of Christian Arabs who have fled Bethlehem, Nablus, Ramallah, and all other places where Muslims dominate—a flight rarely reported. Unsurprisingly, the Christians who have not yet departed blame the Israelis for this displacement, not the Muslim extremists under whose threats of reprisal they live. As for the fate of Jews in the orbit of this self-declared Muslim imperium, the current roar of "resistance to occupation" is notoriously belied by the bloody Arab pogroms of 1920, 1921, 1929, 1936, and 1939, when there was no Jewish state at all, let alone any issue of "settlements." The 1929 attacks left Hebron, the site of an ancient and uninterrupted Jewish community, effectively Judenrein.

What use is there, in the face of brute political and cultural intransigence, to rehearse the events of 1948? In that year Arab rejection of an independent Palestinian state under the UN partition plan led to the invasion by five Arab armies intent on crushing nascent Jewish sovereignty; whole sections of Jerusalem were destroyed or overrun. Nineteen-forty-eight marked the second, though not the first or the last,

Arab refusal of Palestinian statehood. The first came in 1937, when under the British Mandate the Peel Commission proposed partition and statehood for the Arabs of Palestine; the last, and most recent, occurred in 2000, when Arafat dismissed statehood in favor of a well-prepared and programmatic violence. (The flouting of the Road Map by Palestinian unwillingness to dismantle terror gangs will have counted as the Palestinians' fourth refusal of statehood; but the Road Map's callously criminalizing equation of civilian inhabitants of Jewish towns—settlements—with Palestinian murder of Jewish civilians is itself egregious.) After 1948, the Arab war against the Jews of Israel continued through the terror incursions of 1956, the Six-Day War of 1967, the Yom Kippur attacks of 1973, and the fomented violence of 1987, the so-called first intifada.

In short, for two-thirds of a century the Arabs have warred against a Jewish presence in "their" part of the world. The 1967 war in defense of Jewish lives (when affected Jews everywhere went into mourning, fearing catastrophe) culminated in Golda Meir's attempt to return, in exchange for peace, the territories which, in the spirit of partition, Israel had never sought to acquire, and had so unexpectedly conquered. The answer came at an Arab summit in Khartoum: no negotiations, no recognition, no peace. So much for the "crime" of occupation.

And though the Oslo accords of 1993 strove yet again for negotiations, most energetically under Ehud Barak, both the Palestinian leadership and the Palestinian public chose killing over compromise—this time with newly conceived atrocities through suicide bombings, always directed against civilians, in buses, cafés, restaurants, supermarkets, or wherever Israelis peacefully congregate.

This is the history that is ignored or denigrated or distorted or spitefully misrepresented. And because it is a history that has been assaulted and undermined by worldwide falsehoods in the mouths of pundits and journalists, in Europe and all over the Muslim world, the distinction between anti-Semitism and anti-Zionism has finally and utterly collapsed. It is only sophistry, disingenuousness, and corrupted conscience that continue to insist on such a distinction. To fail to trace the pernicious consistencies of Arab political aims from 1920 until today, despite temporary pretensions otherwise, is to elevate intellectual negligence to a principle. To transmogrify self-defense into aggression is to invite an Orwellian horse-laugh. To identify occupation as Israel's primal sin— the most up-to-date Hep! of all—is to be blind to Arab actions and intentions before 1967, and to be equally blind to Israel's repeated commitments to negotiated compromise. On the Palestinian side, the desire to eradicate Jewish nationhood increases daily: it is as if 1948 has returned, replicated in the guise of fanatical young "martyrs" systematically indoctrinated in kindergartens and schools and camps—concerning whom it is cant to say, as many do, that they strap detonators to their loins because they are without hope. It is hope that inflames them.

Perhaps the most bizarre display of international anti-Semitism was flaunted at Durban, during a UN conference ostensibly called to condemn "Racism, Discrimination, Xenophobia, and Related Intolerance." Plucked from the refuse heap, the old UN canard, "Zionism is racism," together with a determined Arab hijacking of the agenda, brought about the bitterest irony of all: a virulent hatred under the auspices of anti-hatred. At Durban the Jewish state was declared to have been conceived in infamy, Jewish representatives were threatened, and language was violated more savagely than at any time since the Nazi era. "Political language," said Orwell, "is designed to make lies sound truthful and murder respectable, and to give the appearance of solidity to pure wind." Yet the rant that emerged at Durban—those instantly recognizable snarls of anti-Semitism—hardly merited the term "political." It had the venerable sound of the mob: Hep! Hep! Hep!

Anti-Semitism is a foolish word; we appear to be stuck with it. "Semitism" has virtually no meaning. The Semites are a linguistic group encompassing Hebrew, Akkadian, Amharic, and Arabic. Anti-Semitism (a term fabricated a century ago by a euphemistic German anti-Semite) signifies hatred of Jews, and hatred's easy corollary: a steady drive to weaken, to hurt, and to extirpate Jews.

Still, one must ask: why the Jews? A sad old joke pluckily confronts the enigma:

—The Jews and the bicyclists are at the bottom of all the world's ills.
—Why the bicyclists?
—Why the Jews?
. . . which implies that blaming one set of irrelevancies is just as irrational as blaming the other. Ah, but it is never the bicyclists, and it is always the Jews.

There are innumerable social, economic, and political speculations as to cause: scapegoatism; envy; exclusionary practices; the temptation of a demographic majority to subjugate a demographic minority; the attempt by corrupt rulers to deflect attention from the failings of their tyrannical regimes; and more.

But any of these can burst out in any society against any people—

so why always the Jews? A metaphysical explanation is proffered: the forceful popular resistance to what Jewish civilization represents—the standard of ethical monotheism and its demands on personal and social conscience. Or else it is proposed, in Freudian terms, that Christianity and Islam, each in its turn, sought to undo the parent religion, which was seen as an authoritative rival it was needful to surpass and displace.

This last notion, however, has no standing in contemporary Christianity. In nearly all Christian communities, there is remorse for the old theologically instigated crimes, and serious internal moral restitution, much of it of a very high order. But a salient fact remains, perhaps impolitic to note: relief has come through Christianity's having long been depleted of temporal power. Today's Islamists, by contrast, are supported and succored by states: Iran, Syria (and Lebanon, its vassal), Saudi Arabia, Sudan, Libya, Malaysia, Indonesia, Pakistan, Egypt (which suppresses its domestic extremists, while its official press, film industry, and other institutions encourage anti-Zionist incitements). Iranian weapons flood into Gaza, whether by sea or through tunnels from Egypt. Saudi Arabia not long ago unashamedly broadcast a telethon to collect millions to be sent to Palestinian terror gangs; it continues today as Hamas's chief funder. And though Saddam Hussein is finally gone, it will not be forgotten that he honored and enriched the families of suicide bombers. (I observe a telltale omission: those who deny any linkage between Iraq and terror universally discount Saddam's lavish payments to Hamas and Islamic Jihad.)

But if one cannot account for the tenacity of anti-Semitism, one can readily identify it. It wears its chic disguises. It breeds on the tongues of liars. The lies may be noisy and primitive and preposterous, like the widespread Islamist charge (doggerelized by New Jersey's poet laureate) that a Jewish conspiracy leveled the Twin Towers. Or the lies may take the form of skilled patter in a respectable timbre, while retailing sleight-of-hand trickeries—such as the hallucinatory notion that the defensive measures of a perennially beleaguered people constitute colonization and victimization; or that the Jewish state is to blame for the aggressions committed against it. Lies shoot up from the rioters in Gaza and Ramallah. Insinuations ripple out of the high tables of Oxbridge. And steadily, whether from the street or the salon, one hears the enduring old cry: Hep! Hep! Hep!

As I write, fresh news arrives—evidence of the fulfillment of one martyr's hope. An Israeli doctor and his twenty-year-old daughter have this day been blown up together in a café, where they had gone for a father-daughter talk on the eve of the young woman's marriage. She had been devoting her year of national service to the care of children with cancer; her ambition was to study medicine for the sake of such children. Her father was an eminent and remarkable physician, the tireless head of a hospital emergency room which tends the victims of terror attacks. He had just returned from the United States, where he was instructing American doctors in the life-saving emergency techniques he had pioneered. Father and daughter were buried on what was to have been the daughter's wedding day.

Cynthia Ozick is the author of many books, among them the novels The Messiah of Stockholm *and* The Shawl. *She has written in* Portland Magazine *of Christian courage in the Holocaust and of God's love; that latter essay appears in* God Is Love, *a collection of the best spiritual essays from* Portland Magazine, *proceeds of which go to scholarships on The Bluff.* "Hep! . . . " *is drawn from a longer essay in the book* Those Who Forget the Past: The Question of Anti-Semitism, *edited by Ron Rosenbaum.*

One of a Kind and All the Same
Notes on hate and love and possibility.

Thomas Lynch

NOT ONLY DID THEY DIE, they disappeared, our dead that day, September 11. There's the terrible fact of the matter. We never got them back to let them go again, to wake and weep over them, to look upon their ordinary loveliness once more, to focus all uncertainties on the awful certainty of a body in a box in a familiar room, borne on shoulders, processed through towns, as if the borderless courtiers of grief and rage could be handled and contained, as if it had a manageable size and shape and weight and matter, as if it could be mapped or measured. But we never got them back. There are thousands dead and gone, God help us.

We know this the way we know the weather and the date and dull facts of happenstance we are helpless to undo. There are many thousand bits and pieces, salvaged from the Fresh Kills landfill site. Families keep vigil at the city morgue. Good news is when they get their portion of the precious body back.

In the papers this April is the image of a man kissing the skull that was found in the dirt of a shallow grave outside a prison in the city of Baghdad. The number on the grave corresponds to the number in the gravedigger's log and the names of the people who are tallied there. The name and the number and the grave and the skull belonged to the man's son. He was taken away years ago. There is a hole in the back of the skull the size of a bullet. There is a letter of other bones, femurs, and ribs, and the man in the photo is strangely pleased.

This is the seeing, hard as it is, that is believing. It is certainty against which the senses rail and to which the senses cling. This is the singular, particular sadness that must be subtracted from the tally of sadness. The globe is littered with such graves as these, people killed by others of their kind, by hate or rage or indifference. Most of the graves will never be found and the dead wander in and out of life never here and never really gone. Whether they are victims of famine, atrocity, terrorism, casualties of a widespread war, part of a national or global tragedy, they are no less spouses and parents, daughters and sons, dear to friends, neighbors, and fellow workers; they are not only missed in the general sense but missed in their particular flesh—in beds, at desks and dinner tables, over drinks and talk and intimacies—the one and only face and voice and touch and being that have ceased to be. And their deaths, like their lives, belong to the precious few before they belong to the history of the world.

Six months after the towers fell, I am in New York City at the invitation of David Posner, senior rabbi at Temple Emanu-El, the largest Jewish house of worship in the world. He has asked me to speak on the Book of Job. I rise early and go for a morning walk, drawn to what has come to be called Ground Zero. I walk down Broadway to Fulton Street, where a viewing platform has been constructed so people can look over Church Street at the gaping wound. Some days, twenty-five thousand people come, lining up like mourners at a wake, for a look. They have to see. The recently constructed ramp is for people to queue up alongside St. Paul's Chapel, with its churchyard of eighteenth- and nineteenth-century stones. George Washington prayed here after his inauguration. It is Manhattan's oldest public building in continuous use. There is a broad deck facing east from which groups of maybe twenty can take a look at what isn't there. It has become, in most ways, negative space. Cameras click into the open air. Men in hard hats work below, in the pit, in the massive open mass grave. Everything stops when "something" is found. Something flag-draped and horizontal is carried slowly up out of the hole to an ambulance. Work resumes. On the boardwalk that leads back to Broadway, there is a wall on which the names of the dead are listed alphabetically. It begins with Gordon Aamoth and ends with Igor Zukelman. There are Murrays and McMahons, Collinses and Keanes, Curtins, Maloneys, and Mahoneys, all names of my neighbors in County Clare and names from the far-flung and neighboring townlands: Doherty, Dolan, Doyle, Crotty, and Curry. Like the dead, the Irish are everywhere. And when I come to the Lynches in this grim litany, I am shocked to see the names of my own boys, Sean and Michael.

I count them all: Farrell Peter Lynch, James Francis Lynch, Louise

A. Lynch, Michael Lynch, and Sean P. Lynch. Ten of them—a bond trader, a property manager, stockbrokers, firemen, and cops; and two brothers of immigrants who worked together at Cantor Fitzgerald. One over fifty, two over forty, the rest in their thirties, primes of their lives, all murdered in the one madness, in the same sixteen-acre killing field at the south end of an island city of the world between 8:46 and 10:28 on a Tuesday morning. The only name with more murdered there was *Smith*. There are a dozen Smiths. There are ten Kellys, too—James and Joseph and Richard and three Toms—and ten Murphys—Raymond and John, Joe, Edward, and Kevin and strangely, as I read it, no Michaels or Seans. In all, sixty-four names that begin with "Mc"—McAleese and McCourt, and McSweeneys. Four O'Briens, four O'Connors, one O'Callaghan, two O'Keefes, and O'Grady, O'Hagan, O'Sheas, and O'Neils. Oh God, it seems so Irish and American. So very sad and beautiless. It seems like a chapter from the Book of Job.

We humans have these troubles everywhere. Religion, race, and nationality; gender, age, affiliations—these define and divide us. We are ennobled and estranged by them. These "conditions" are, unfashionably, not matters of choice. I am Catholic in the way I am white and American and male and middle-aged—irreversibly, inexorably, inexcusably. However lapsed or lazy or lacking in faith I am on any given day, I am, at the same time, a lapsed, lazy, and faithless Catholic. I sin and am forgiven according to the language I learned as a child—a dialect of shalts and shalt-nots, blessings and beatitudes, curses and prejudices. Surely it is no different for the children of observant Jews, Muslims, Methodists, and secular humanists. Religion is the double-edged sword that unites, protects, and secures while it divides and conquers and endangers, always and ever in the names of God, the subtextual message of all religions is that, while we are all God's children, God likes some of his children better than others, and that heaven, wherever it turns out to be, will be populated by those of one kind and not another.

Of course in Belfast, as in Baghdad or Jerusalem, the issue isn't doctrine or observance. There are fewer true believers than we like to think, and true believers honor true belief in others even when it is not a belief they share. The issue is otherness. How we separate ourselves from other human kinds. Religion is just one of the several easy ways for the blessed and elect to remain just that. The haves and the have-nots around the world maintain their status—as victimizer and aggrieved—on the narrowest grounds of difference. Race, religion, tribe, caste, class, club, color, gender, sexual preference, denomination, sect, geography, and politics—everything we are separates us from everyone else. In the border counties of Ulster, where it is hard to tell Kenneth from Sean, or Alison from Mary, where everyone is fair and freckled, "he digs with the wrong foot" and "she has squinty eyes" are both the sublime and the ridiculous truth. It is the same in Baghdad, where it is impossible to say who is Sunni and who is Shiite, who is Baathist and who is not. Everyone on the news looks the same to me. Does it have something to do with the headgear, the eyes? What's in a name? Everyone here is Muhammad or Ali.

Last year I read in the *Irish Times* about Muhammad Ali's Irish roots. Antoinette O'Brien of the Clare Heritage Centre in Corofin had traced the connections.

Was there ever any doubt?

"The Greatest," it will come as no surprise to Claremen and Clarewomen round the planet, has roots in the Banner County. Like my great-grandfather, Ali's great-grandfather came from that poor country bordered by the River Shannon and the North Atlantic, famous for poets and dancers and knock-down handsome men who float like butterflies and sting like bees.

"Up Clare!" is the only thing to be said about it.

Born in the gray city of Ennis in the 1840s, as grim a decade as ever was, Abe Grady left for the New World in his twenties. He got the boat at Cappa Pier by Kilrush—not ten miles upriver from my ancestral hovel in Moveen—and made west for The Better Life.

Mr. Grady found his way to Kentucky, where he was smitten, in circumstances undocumented by Ms. O'Brien, like men of the species since time began, by the dark beauties of an African woman. Like my great-grandfather, in his youth Abe had never seen a visage that wasn't freckled, blue-eyed, pale-faced, and blushed-red. Little wonder that he found her lovely and exotic, enchanting altogether.

A son of their union, an African Irish American, it was reported, also married a black woman, and one of their daughters, Odessa Lee Grady, married Cassius Marcellus Clay the elder in the 1930s and settled in Louisville, where the Greatest, formerly known as Cassius Marcellus Clay, Junior, was born to them on January 17, 1942.

The world, of course, has been the better for it.

The Champ, who like me lives in Michigan, has not said when he intends to return to the country of his ancestors.

History is a sad and instructive study. The County Clare that Abe Grady left was, per capita, the most decimated by emigration of any county in Ireland. They did not leave as tourists. They left like the Jews of Europe left a century later for Israel—withered, starving, having just survived. They left like Somalis and Iraqis and Cherokees and Bosnians, because they had no choice. For most emigrant Irish of the nineteenth century, the choice was fairly simple: stay and starve, surely, or leave and maybe live, maybe. Abe, we might imagine, was in the same circumstances.

Ali's great-grandmother's people came as slaves, in boats built in Belfast, like the one that Abe took down the Shannon and across the sea. Colonization, abject poverty, forced emigration by starvation, eviction, and political domination—all close and distant cousins, of a kind—bondage done up in the Sunday dress of steerage, slavers turned into coffin ships, the human cargo stacked like chattel in the hold, a third of them dead en route or on landing, all of them well below tourist class, all of them looking for a class of people worse off than themselves.

The smaller the world gets, the greater the hatreds seem. April this year is full of unseasonable weather. The Jews are celebrating Passover; the Christians, Easter. The Shiite Muslims in Iran and Iraq are making their pilgrimage to Karbala by the hundreds of thousands. They are going to the tomb of Hussein, the founder of their sect and grandson of the Prophet Muhammad, who was murdered by Sunnis 1,400 years ago, the way Christians say Christ was by Romans and Jews. For twenty-five years it was forbidden, under the rule of Saddam Hussein, for Shiite Muslims to make the pilgrimage, to observe the holy days of atonement, self-flagellation, chest thumping, and ritual sacrifices of lambs in commemoration of an event equivalent to the Crucifixion of Christ for the Christians. The Shiites are thanking God for the end of Saddam Hussein and calling for the infidel Americans to leave. The clerics are jockeying for position.

In Ireland they are marking the anniversary of the Good Friday Agreement by which, in 1998, all of the hateful parties to the Troubles gathered in a room to sort out how to organize their hates into a manageable government. As a friend of mine, born in Fermanagh, living in London with her husband and children, said, "Peace has broken out in my country!"

Maybe this is what the president's speechwriter meant when he or she wrote that Ireland gives hope for Iraq—that while we have no choice about our hateful natures, we can sit great hatreds down in the one room and organize a peace. We can seize this from the other possibilities. The themes of slavery and liberation, death and resurrection, oppression and freedom, sacrifice and miracle, new life, old grudges, pilgrimage and exodus, rage and tolerance are an important study. The world's grim history of apartheid and ethnic cleansing, holocaust and resettling, jihad and forced migration is blight upon our human nature. What Oliver Cromwell did to the Irish in the seventeenth century, the ethnic cleansing, required him to see the slaughter of Irish peasants and their forced resettlement in the barren West as "the judgment of God on these barbarous wretches." Our species has not evolved much past such evil.

In 1953, James Watson and Francis Crick proposed the double-helix molecular structure of DNA. In 1990, the Human Genome Project took up its ambition to map the DNA structure of human beings. It turns out that we are, each and every one of us, one of a kind and all the same. Mother Teresa and Adolf Hitler have much in common. George Custer and Catherine of Siena, Mandela and Milosevic are genetically much the same. We all trace our mitochondrial roots to an Eve in Tanzania 150,000 years ago. The Mother of All Humans adrift in the world.

Thomas Lynch is the author of the superb books The Undertaking *and* Booking Passage, *among others.*

THE CLOSEST TO LOVE WE EVER GET

Maybe the noisy song we make all together is the most powerful prayer of all.

HEATHER KING

There is another world, and it is this one. —Paul Eluard

I'M A PERSON WHO CRAVES QUIET and solitude, yet I've lived in the crowded, noisy Los Angeles neighborhood of Koreatown for eleven years. I tell myself it's because I have a spacious, beautiful apartment and a gated courtyard filled with hibiscus and pomegranates. I tell myself it's because I pay only $760 a month—half as much as almost anywhere else in the city. But the longer I stay, the more I see it's not just the apartment that keeps me here: it's the challenges, the dilemmas, the paradoxes. People blast ranchera music at three in the morning but they also prune bougainvillea into glories of cascading blooms. They spraypaint gang slogans on my garage door by night and scrub the sidewalks clean by day. As I hang out my clothes on the line by the lemon tree, my back is to a busted washing machine; across the alley, a brand-new down comforter, still in its package, sits on top of a dumpster.

Part of my impulse living here is to hide out from the rest of the city—from the cell phones and SUVs, the hipsters, the people writing screenplays in too-cool-to-care coffeehouses—but in Koreatown I can't hide out from myself. Here I come face-to-face every day with the cross of my irritation, my anger, my racism, my fear. Here I am plunged into the deepest contradictions: between abundance and scarcity, community and solitude, sin and grace, my longing for wholeness and my resistance to it.

Here, I have no voice, no particular power. At Mass at St. Basil's, at 24-Hour Fitness, at Charlie Chan's Printing, at Ralph's Grocery, at the Vietnamese shop where I get my pedicures, I am often the only white person present. When I call out my window to Jung, the kid next door, to keep it down, he yells back: "We were here first! Why don't you move?" His 9-year-old face contorted by hate; hurt and fury rising in my own throat; I don't have to read the headlines on Iraq to know how wars start, how the battle lines are drawn. I have driven from Koreatown to Death Valley, to Anza Borrego, to the East Mojave. I am pulled to the desert as if by a magnet; I'm forever scheming to escape there for a week, or two, or a month; I devour books about the desert, and yet I am uneasy with the "nature" writers who leave human beings out, who see us as a blight on the landscape. As a human being, and a Catholic, I see the cross everywhere: in actual deserts and, in the middle of one of the most densely populated sections of Los Angeles, in the desert of my own conflicted heart. Living in Koreatown has fortified my sense of apartness, allowed me to be in the city but not always of it, shaped me as a writer. But a writer has to be fully engaged: emotionally, spiritually, physically; has to mingle his or her body and blood with the rest of the world, the people in it, the page; has to find a way to cherish that world even as he or she struggles to endure it—Flannery O'Connor's phrase— which is perhaps the best definition of the cross I know. How can you be Catholic?, people ask, and I want to ask back, but am afraid to, how can you write unless in some sense you have died and been resurrected and, in one way or another, are burning to tell people about it? How can you bear the sorrow of a world in which every last thing passes away without knowing that Christ is right up there on the cross with you?

How can you be spiritual in L.A.?, someone from back East once asked and, as a car alarm blared, a leafblower blasted, and I looked out my window at the children hanging out the windows of the six-story apartment building across the street and screaming, I thought, how can you deal with this ceaselessly pulsing aorta of life with anything but spirituality?

Sometimes I have coffee with my friend Joan, who waitresses at Langer's Deli, or my friend Larry, a janitor at Kaiser. Here is what feeds me: sitting on the corner of Wilshire and Serrano with traffic streaming by while Joan tells me about her troubles with the cook at work, or Larry, who did time at every mental health facility from Camarillo to Norwalk before he stopped drinking, reminisces about his "nuthouse romances." What feeds me is the miracle of flesh-and-blood, of stories, of the daily struggles that "break, blow, burn" and make us new, as John Donne put it, that give us compassion for the struggles of others.

Inching out into Oxford Avenue on foot, headed to the library, I can barely make it across, there are so many cars barreling down from either direction: honking, cutting each other off, jostling for space. It's so easy to feel besieged, so easy to think why are there so many of them instead of realizing I'm one of "them" myself; that nobody else likes being crowded either. How can a person live a life of love? I ask myself as I reach the opposite curb: not love tacked on, added as an afterthought, but shot through every second; flaming out, "like shining from shook foil," as Gerard Manley Hopkins described the grandeur of God.

Wending my way home with my books, my vision temporarily transformed, I'm not seeing the refrigerators abandoned on the sidewalk, the triple-parked ice cream trucks, the overflowing trash cans. I'm seeing flashes of colorful Mexican tile, the 98-cent store mural of waltzing Ajax cans and jitterbugging mops, my favorite flowers: the heliotrope on Ardmore, the wisteria near Harvard, the lemon on Mariposa. Or maybe it's not that I'm seeing one group of things instead of another, but for one fleeting moment, all simultaneously: the opposites held in balance a paradigm for the terrible tension and ambiguity of the human condition; the dreadful reality that we can never quite be sure which things we have done and which things we have failed to do, the difference between how we long for the world to be and how it must be a kind of crucifixion in the darkest, most excruciating depths of which we discover—the rear windows of the parked cars I'm walking by now covered with jacaranda blossoms—it's not that there's not enough beauty; it's that there's so much it can hardly be borne.

Monday morning, putting out the garbage as the sky turns pink above the salmon stucco façades, I bend my face to the gardenia in the courtyard, knowing that every shabby corner, every bird and flower and blade of grass, every honking horn and piece of graffiti, every pain and contradiction, deserves a song of praise. O Sacrament most holy, O Sacrament divine . . . , we sang at Mass yesterday. The kids are coming in droves now, making their way to Hobart Middle School—pushing, yelling, throwing their candy wrappers on the sidewalk—and that is a kind of hymn, too. We're all doing our part, their exuberant shouts mingling with the thoughts I'll shape into an essay, all drifting like incense, raised aloft and offered up to the smoggy air above Koreatown. Maybe that's exactly as it should be. Maybe I need their noise and they need my silence; maybe the song we make together—all of us—is the closest to love we ever get.

"What are we here for?" Annie Dillard asks in *The Writing Life.* "Propter chorum, the monks say: for the sake of the choir."

Heather King is the author of Parched: A Memoir, *among other books.*

WE HAVE ALWAYS BEEN HERE

An Umatilla woman ponders the Corps of Discovery.

ROBERTA CONNER

THE WALLA WALLA, UMATILLA, and Cayuse Tribes, as we are now known, make up the Confederated Tribes of the Umatilla Indian Reservation just east of Pendleton, Oregon. There are some 2,470 enrolled members in our Confederacy, up from 1,100 in the 1880s, yet well below the estimated 8,000 at the time we met the Corps of Discovery.

October 19, 1805. The great chief Yel-lep-pit [and other chiefs] presented themselves to us very early this morning. we Smoked with them, enformed them as we had all others above as well as we Could by Signs of our friendly intentions towards our red children Perticular those who opened their ears to our Councils. . . . They said we came from the clouds . . . and were not men &c &c.—William Clark

Our people have always been here. How long is always? As far back as our stories recall. Back to when the landforms were created, back to the end of the cold times, back to the floods, back to the times when the mountains hurled rocks and fire at each other, back to when the animals held council and taught us how to live here. From the animals, plants, waterways, and the cycles provided by the seasons, we learned what to eat, where to live at different times of the year, how to heal ourselves and take care of one another. Our traditional laws, still in place, never replaced or superseded, tell us how to take care of the gifts from the Creator. In our cultures, children are sacred as are all the beings made by the Creator. That is the ages-old context into which Lewis and Clark arrived in 1805. By virtue of them saying so, these newcomers proclaimed we were children to their Great Father. Not so. We are children of this landscape.

When the Lewis and Clark Expedition traveled through the mid-Columbia Plateau, this land was ours. This was not part of the young United States. While Russia, Spain, France, Britain, and the United States imagined the potential of economic control over abundant resources and trade with western tribes that would follow exploration, they exerted no control here. Protected by the Rocky Mountains to the east, the Blue Mountains to the south, and the Cascades to the west as well as the Columbia River narrows and falls, only native peoples lived here. We traded for white men's goods, we knew of them through our travels, and our prophecies foretold their arrival. But our local way of life was not threatened by their passage through our homeland. Thirty-three travelers were a curiosity, a trade opportunity.

The peoples Lewis and Clark called Wallahwollah call themselves Waluulapam. "Walla Walla" describes the many small flows of water that braid their way to the main stem of the Columbia River in that area. More than likely, their two Nez Perce escorts informed the expedition of the name of the waterway and then the Corps applied that name to the people. Today, the Cayuse language is extinct, save about 400 documented words, and most Cayuse descendants who speak a native language speak lower or upper Nez Perce. The few persons who speak Walla Walla as a first language are all elders. Those who speak Umatilla as a first language are a handful of adults and a few elders. Lewis and Clark heard at least three languages on October 16 at the confluence of the Snake and Columbia Rivers. That they did not know precisely which ones, or did not have the time to find out, is not important. What is important is the knowledge that is embedded in our tribal languages that accurately and efficiently tells the history of the ecosystems of the Columbia River drainage system.

In his second inaugural address on March 4, 1805, President Jefferson observed: "These persons inculcate a sanctimonious reverence for the customs of their ancestors; that whatsoever they did, must be done through all time; that reason is a false guide, and advance under its counsel, in their physical, moral, or political condition, is perilous innovation; that their duty is to remain as their Creator made them, ignorance being safety, and knowledge full of danger. . . ."

Today, our people persist in resembling the observation regarding our sanctimonious reverence for the customs of our ancestors. It would be unwise to do otherwise. After thousands of years on this landscape, their empirical knowledge should be revered. This reverence for the ancient covenant between our people and salmon, for example, resulted in the ethic that one should never take all of anything in harvest. Always leave fish to pass up river, roots for others, berries for the other species who eat them. This same ancient covenant led the modern Confederated Tribes of Umatilla to undertake extraordinary efforts to successfully restore water flows and salmon to the Umatilla and Walla Walla Rivers.

Our homeland was neither an unoccupied frontier nor a wilderness. In fact, the concept of wilderness does not directly translate into our languages because it is a foreign construct. The journey from what is now North Dakota to what is now Oregon included contact with many tribal peoples. When the expedition arrived in the Columbia River Plateau, they entered one of the most populous areas they had been in since leaving the Mandan villages. And the Mandan villages, despite decimation by disease, were more densely populated than St. Louis, then a western outpost. The Corps of Discovery's "western estimate of Indians" included 114 tribes that are now represented by at least 58 modern tribal nations. Their estimate, while incomplete, included about 4,700 estimated "soles" that were ancestors to the tribes now in our confederation of Cayuse, Umatilla, and Walla Walla.

October 19th Saturday 1805 The great chief Yel-lep-pit two other chiefs . . . presented themselves to us verry early this morning. . . . Yelleppit is a bold handsom Indian, with a dignified countenance about 35 years of age, about 5 feet 8 inches high and well perpotiond. he requested us to delay untill the Middle of the day, that his people might Come down and See us. . . . great numbers of Indians Came down in Canoes to view us before we Set out. . . . —William Clark

Lewis and Clark were an attraction when they arrived in our homeland in 1805. One of our leaders twice entreated them to stay longer so that more of his people may come and see them. One of our elders was told that her ancestors had found the men of the expedition peculiar because they appeared to be eating themselves—the men would reach into their breeches and pull something out to eat. They had pockets, which our people did not, in their leggings or pants. That people came by the hundreds to view the expedition is evidence of the effectiveness of the moccasin telegraph and suggests just how peculiar and novel these travelers were.

20th of April 1806 . . . all the Indians we have Seen play a game &
risque all the property they have at different games. the game that these
Savages play is by setting in a circle & have a Small Smooth bone in
their hands & Sing crossing their hands to fix it in a hidden manner
from the other Side who gass the hand that has it in then counts one a
Stick Stuck in the ground for the tallies & So on untill one Side or the
other wins the property Stacked up. this game is play with activity, and
they appear merry & peaceable. Capt. Lewis took the property from
the man that gambled away our horse. . . . the Indians would not give
us any thing worth mentioning for our canoes So we Split & burnt one
of them this evening. —John Ordway

Varied games and forms of gambling have been used for centuries,
if not longer, to redistribute wealth along the Columbia River. Lewis
and Clark apparently wanted to engage in trade straight away but
did not wish to use their canoe to gamble for what they might obtain
in a more time-consuming and chancy manner. But one of the men
of the expedition did take a turn and lost a horse and then lost the
gains from gambling to the Captain. That gambling is inappropriate
in any way is not our cultural conclusion. That judgment arrives with
the missionaries. In today's world, roughly 40% of federally recognized tribes use gaming as a means to an end. Without the benefit of
a significant tax base to fund essential government services, tribes use
the net profits from gaming to provide fire, police, sanitation, and
emergency medical services as well as education, youth care, and elder
care among other services. Gaming also provides jobs and incomes on
reservations where unemployment previously stagnated for decades
between 40 and 80 percent.

April 28th 1806 . . . we found a Shoshone woman, prisoner among
these people by means of whome and Sahcahgarweah we found the
means of conversing with the Wollah-wollahs. . . . —Meriwether Lewis

Tribal practices included taking captives during raids on neighboring
rivals. The captive or slave station in the family and community were
not necessarily permanent. A captive could ascend to higher stature by
excelling, demonstrating worth to the community and proving commit-
ment to the people. York, for example, given his skills and record of
service to Clark, would likely have fared better amongst Indians. For us,
raids were a means of obtaining goods, livestock, and productive labor

from those with whom we did not routinely trade. Raids and warfare were not conducted for the purpose of annihilation of another people. It would be counterproductive to completely eliminate another people.

October 17th 1805 . . . This river is remarkably Clear and Crouded with Salmon in maney places, I observe in assending great numbers of Salmon dead on the Shores, floating on the water and in the Bottoms which can be seen at the debth of 20 feet. the Cause of the emence numbers of dead Salmon I can't account for So it is I must have seen 3 or 400 dead and maney living. . . . —William Clark

We were resident; Lewis and Clark and all members of the Expedition were transient. They saw much that they did not comprehend, even when they tried in earnest to understand. In fact, as they traveled President Jefferson's expansionist fantasy seeking a direct water route through the continent, they were exploring the place the Creator gave us to live. The Creator gave everyone a place to live. Why were they in our country, living precariously in a place they did not belong? Moreover, why would our ancestors be so hospitable to these strangers? Why not? They were 33 travelers merely passing through who did not represent a threat to our way of life at the time of their passing and for years to come. Could anyone foresee that 109 years later dams on the Umatilla River would prevent fish passage and that our Tribes would have to work for years to return water to the riverbed and reintroduce salmon to the Umatilla River after an absence of 70 years? Did anyone envision that 152 years later, the richest salmon fishery in the West, the magnificent Celilo Falls, would be submerged under the backwaters of The Dalles Dam? That Lewis and Clark were unfamiliar with the anadromous fish teeming in the rivers—fresh with just as many spawned out lying dead—is not important. What is important is our modern challenge to protect water flows and salmon habitat and restore salmon runs not to 1950s pre-dam levels, but to the levels that Lewis and Clark indubitably witnessed.

April 28th 1806 . . . a little before Sun Set the Chim nah poms arrived. . . . they joined the Wallah wallahs . . . and formed a half circle arround our camp. . . . the whole assemblage of Indians about 350 men women and Children Sung and danced at the Same time. most of them danced in the Same place they Stood and mearly jumped up to the time of their musick. Some of the men who were esteemed most brave

entered the Space around which the main body were formed in Solid
Column and danced in a Circular manner Side wise. at 10 P M. the dance
ended and the nativs retired; they were much gratified in Seeing Some of
our Party join them in their dance. one of their party who made himself
the most Conspicious Charecter in the dance and Songs, we were told
was a Medesene man & Could foretell things. that he had told of our
Comeing into their Country and was now about to consult his God the
moon if what we Said was the truth &c. &c. —William Clark

We had philosophy, laws, order, and religion; we were not uncivilized
or wild. We lived according to our laws in the order established in our
homes and homeland. Our law emanated from our ecosystem and our
philosophy and is celebrated in our music. On the night of April 28,
1806, the members of the expedition did not distinguish the kinds of
songs and dances they witnessed. As native people read what was written, we recognize that they are describing a worship service in which
each song is a prayer and they are participating in a ceremony in which
the fulfillment of the prophecy of the new people coming is proclaimed.
It is a Washat service. Our people still sing the prayer songs that were
likely sung that night. In our longhouses, people still mark time to the
prayer songs and dance jumping in time to the music in a circular side-
ways manner as described 200 years ago. Elders here have spoken of the
announcement of the fulfillment of the prophecy. That Clark thought
the medicine man was consulting the moon is not far from the errone-
ous notion assumed by the traders who later occupied Fort Nez Perces
at Wallula—that we were sun worshipers. In actuality, the practice of
greeting the day in prayer at sunrise facing east led to this conclusion
that we worship the Creator, the supreme light of the world, maker of
all, in all our prayers.

April 26th 1806 . . . we were over taken to day by Several families of
the nativs who were traveling up the river with a Numr. of horses; they
Continued with us much to our ennoyance as the day was worm the
roads dusty and we Could not prevent their horses Crouding in and
breaking our order of March without useing Some acts of Severty which
we did not wish to Commit. —William Clark

Although our once great horse culture is now a remnant of what it once
was, it is not gone. After our homeland became a "fur desert" as otter
and beaver were obliterated for a hat craze in "civilized" nations, horses

were our stock in trade. Our selective breeding practices yielded fast, hearty horses renowned for their stamina and soundness. A few of our famously sturdy, fast equine went to Bora Bora during World War II. By the 1950s, farming, ranching, and railroads find horses a nuisance and post-depression economics and the auto result in thousands of horses being "canned" for dog food and glue. Nonetheless, within our modern tribes are people who rodeo, race horses, rope, trail ride, teach horsemanship, cut, rein, round up cattle and hunt horseback. Canoe making has ceased but threatens resurgence because other neighboring tribes have maintained this skill. Many of the tribal technologies that sustained our people for millennia continue because they are valuable—not as quaint traditions—but as knowledge of our universe. Hunting, fish harvest, root digging, and associated processing technologies represent ways of perpetuating the sacred species given to us on this land. Formal rites of passage for first kill, first fish, first digging, and first picking are still observed in families and in the longhouse. The ways of knowing are as valued as the land and animals that taught our ancestors. Being instructed formally and finding answers from nature are both accepted methods of obtaining knowledge.

April 30th 1806 . . . this plain as usual is covered with arromatic shrubs hurbatious plants and a short grass. many of those plants produce those esculent roots which form a principal part of the subsistence of the natives. among others there is one which produces a root somewhat like the sweet pittaitoe. . . . Drewyer killed a beaver and an otter; a part of the former we reserved for ourselves and gave the indians the ballance. these people will not eat the dog but feast heartily on the otter which is vastly inferior in my estimation, they sometimes also eat their horses, this indeed is common to all the indians who possess this annimal in the plains of Columbia; but it is only done when necessity compells them.
—Meriwether Lewis

Our indigenous diet was lean, rich, and diverse, and our people were physical and athletic (especially compared to today's diabetes-inducing nutrition and lifestyles). Despite their awareness of native plant foods, members of the Expedition ate, according to scholarly estimates, 9 pounds of meat per man per day. If they found Indian customs peculiar and our diet distasteful, imagine what we thought of them. While we did not consume dog, and would only consume horsemeat in a rare circumstance, they preferred these meats to salmon. They bought at least 50 dogs from our camps on the outbound journey. There was no alcohol in our diet. Unlike the expedition, we did not make spirits out of rotting camas roots. And, for regular cleansing, both physical and spiritual, we had our sweathouses and bathed frequently in streams and rivers compared to the members of the expedition, who were, according to tribal oral history, smelly.

1st day of May 1806 . . . some time after we had encamped three young men arived from the Wallahwollah village bringing with them a steel trap belonging to one of our party which had been neglegently left behind; this is an act of integrity rarely witnessed among indians. during our stay with them they several times found knives of the men which had been carelessly lossed by them and returned them. I think we can justly affirm to the honor of these people that they are the most hospitable, honest, and sincere people that we have met with in our voyage.
—Meriwether Lewis

Native peoples were not heathens, thieves, squaw drudges, savages, or even chiefs. While Indians were described as such in the journals of the six men in the Expedition who could write, these were all terms given to us by others outside our cultures that represented common vernacular of the day, albeit largely derogatory. If saying it doesn't make it so, writing it down did not improve the veracity of such labels. When our Niimipu (Nez Perce) relatives escorted them into the mid-Columbia Plateau, the explorers encountered orderly division of labor between genders, picketed graves and burial islands, veneration of elders that was obvious even to outsiders, people unafraid of new commerce opportunities, people who were multilingual and displays of tremendous hospitality. Our people continue to be welcoming, straightforward, and heartfelt in our endeavors and sadly, racial epithets and derogatory labels persist.

Our tribes were sovereign nations when President Jefferson dispatched the expedition. We were nations at the Walla Walla Treaty Council in 1855. We are nations today. Lewis and Clark carried the message of U.S. sovereignty to each of the tribal nations they met; diplomacy was part of their directive. During the face-to-face diplomatic overtures of the expedition, no one deliberated our ownership, our occupancy, or our authority. Lewis and Clark had no doubt that they were visitors. But in the "seventeen great nations" on the other coast, and across the Atlantic waters in Europe, unmistakable precedents had already shaped what would become our destiny—manifest destiny borne of the rights of discovery.

"The dispatch of the Lewis and Clark expedition was an act of imperial policy," wrote Bernard DeVoto in *The Course of Empire*. "The United States had embarked on the path of building a transcontinental empire," and the expedition "dramatically enhanced the United States' 'discovery rights' to what became known as the Oregon Country," Stephen Dow Beckham writes in *Lewis & Clark: From the Rockies to the Pacific*. The Lewis and Clark Law School professor Robert Miller has noted that the United States did not actually buy the land in the famous Louisiana Purchase; it bought Napoleon's so-called discoverer's rights. "'Discovery' was applied by European/Americans to legally infringe on the real property and sovereign rights of the American Indian nations and their people, without their knowledge or consent, and it continues to adversely affect Indian tribes and people today," writes Miller.

And Jefferson knew very well what the American Indians faced. "The aboriginal inhabitants of these countries I have regarded with the commiseration their history inspires," he said. "Endowed with the faculties and the rights of men, breathing ardent love of liberty and independence, and occupying a country which left them no desire but to be undisturbed, the stream of overflowing population from other regions directed itself on these shores; without power to divert, or habits to contend against, they have been overwhelmed by the current, or driven before it. . . ."

If members of the Corps knowingly conducted reconnaissance with foresight and intent to dispossess Indians of their lands, should Americans still applaud their journey?

Yes.

The members of the expedition were courageous, observant, astute, conscientious, and diligent about their duties. They were far from home, vastly outnumbered by Indians, and largely uneducated about the lands, conditions, and peoples in the West, but they performed their duties very well indeed. That they were ignorant of the inherent knowledge and values in these ancient cultures does not separate them from many people today. That they were just following orders in preparing for the dispossession of lands from American Indians does not distinguish them from more modern federal emissaries. They were a small military unit, representing a distant, ambitious president leading an immature nation, doing the best they could with what they had in the times and within the mores with which they were born and raised.

The Louisiana Purchase and the Lewis and Clark Expedition shaped the future boundaries of the young United States and changed our peoples' lives forever. Less than 50 years after Lewis and Clark trooped through the middle of the homelands of the Walla Walla, Umatilla, and Cayuse, our leaders ceded, under duress, roughly six million acres of land to the United States. Washington Territorial Governor Isaac Stevens conducted a 14-month campaign to conclude 10 treaties that would yield approximately 70 million acres of the Pacific Northwest to the United States by 1856.

In the same treaty council, Oregon Superintendent of Indian Affairs Joel Palmer says: "It is but fifty years since the first white man came among you, those were Lewis and Clark who came down the Big River—the Columbia . . . then came the Hudson Bay Co. who were traders. Next came missionaries; these were followed by emigrants with wagons across the plains; and now we have a good many settlers in the country below you. . . . Like the grasshoppers on the plains; some years there will be more come than others, you cannot stop them; they say this land was not made for you alone. . . . Who can say that this is mine and that is yours? The white man will come to enjoy these blessings with you; what shall we do to protect you and preserve peace? There are but few whites here now, there will be many, let us like wise men, act so as to prevent trouble. . . . And now while there is room to select for you a home where there are no white men living let us do so. . . ."

Our spokesmen at the Treaty Council were not naïve, nor were they oblivious to the fact that decisions were being made for them without consultation or their consent. At the Council, Cayuse leader Young Chief said, "The reason why we could not understand you was that you selected this country for us to live in without our having any voice in the matter. . . . You embraced all my country, where was I to go, was I to be a wanderer like a wolf. Without a home without a house I would be compelled to steal, consequently I would die. . . . I think the land where my forefathers are buried should be mine."

Walla Walla leader PeoPeoMoxMox: "In one day the Americans become as numerous as the grass; this I learned in California; I know that it is not right. You have spoken in a round about way; speak straight. I have ears to hear you and here is my heart. . . ."

Our fate would be the one common to most Indians in the late 19th century. While some would become successful farmers and ranchers, most of our people would adjust to subsist on the fishing, hunting, gathering, trapping, and grazing rights reserved in our Treaty of

1855, without which our suffering would have been much worse. The government policies and practices in reservation life and boarding schools would further disenfranchise and fractionalize our people, but they would not do us in. We are still working to overcome the social, psychological, physical, and economic consequences of what followed Lewis and Clark. At great cost, our people have survived. In every major tribal decision-making point since, the troubles of our ancestors are revisited. We do not do this to remind ourselves of the injustices. We do so to remind ourselves of the wisdom, fortitude, forbearance, and foresight of our ancestors who made tremendous sacrifices so that we may still be here in our homeland and so that we follow their example.

The story of my people was, is, and always will be this land. The passage of time does not separate us from the land. We are not going to go away or become extinct. This nation is our home. We have been patient. But the land and animals that the Creator placed here with us need our help. The way we all live has consequences for water and air quality and affects all the other creatures with which we share this home. Our imperative is constant: we must protect our home and all the gifts from the Creator.

My grandfather's great-grandfathers were boys when the Lewis and Clark expedition came into our homeland. Those boys would grow up and represent our people at the Walla Walla Treaty Council of 1855. In their lifetimes, the hospitality, sincerity, and honesty of their parents would not save them from the travesty and tragedy of the unsettling of the West. Their tribes went from being superior hosts to Lewis and Clark to being forced to cede all or most of their home away.

Yet "our peoples' devotion to this land is stronger than any piece of paper," my grandfather told my mother, when explaining his First World War tour of duty in France with the Navy long before Indians had the right to vote. That's why he went to war when his nation had conflict with other countries. That devotion to the land we all share is deeper than our mistrust. It is more important than our wounds from past injustices. It is tougher than hatred. It is a gift from the Creator.

Roberta Conner—Sisaawipam, to use her birth name—is Cayuse, Umatilla, and Nez Perce in heritage. She directs the Tamástslikt Cultural Institute of the Confederated Tribes of the Umatilla Reservation in eastern Oregon. Her piece here is excerpted from the book Lewis and Clark through Indian Eyes, *edited by the late, wonderful historian Alvin Josephy of Joseph, Oregon. Our prayers on Alvin's soul. He was a great gentleman.*

Who Am I?

Notes on ecstatic moments.

JOHN COATS

I'VE HAD A NUMBER OF THEM, actually, all unexpected. There was, for example, the moment I came face-to-face with Van Gogh's self-portrait in Paris, the one in which he is without a hat, in which his craziness seems, literally, to radiate off him like rays from the sun. All that mad beauty left me wide open, on the edge of something glorious and transcendent. And there've been other moments of magnitude. But the big one for me came in 1958, a few months after my twelfth birthday, less than a mile from my home, and in a place as foreign to my experience as Pluto.

I'd grown up a Southern Baptist, with its low-church Protestantism, its plain architecture and minimalist sanctuaries. I'd never seen anything like the beauty and vibrancy of the silken, embroidered cloth on St. Paul's altar that day, nor the golden candelabra, nor the statuary, especially Mary, nor what impressed me then as the rather miserable-looking Jesus on the cross above the altar—a far cry from the tepid portraits of Jesus on the walls of our Sunday School rooms. And there was a faint fragrance in the air, something of the place itself, spicy, old, remnant-like, haunting, and mysterious.

My family and I were at St. Paul's for Nuptial Mass. I'd been angry when we'd arrived; it was, after all, the first cold Saturday of autumn, a day for playing football with my buddies, not sitting in church. But all the beauty had surprised me, and I was calmer now, even peaceful. Then the music swelled. People stood, some half-turning toward the back, straining their necks to see, like people waiting for a parade. Curious, I turned and, through the adults, saw a boy holding what appeared to be a brass cross mounted atop a varnished broomstick, and in front of that was a fellow about my age swinging a smoking pot. As they passed, a bit of the smoke wafted toward me, and it was the same scent.

It was like a scene from an old movie when someone remembers the past and the picture dissolves into wavy lines, but this was only in one spot, sort of oval-shaped, and just above and in front of the cross. Then, as if that spot marked a door between here and somewhere else, it seemed to open and close in a blink, like a camera's shutter. I had the sensation of something hitting me in the belly, but not hard. With that, it—whatever it was—was over.

I was aware of a heaviness that had not been there, a numb heartache of the sort I'd felt when my dog died or when a dear friend moved away. As for the rest of the service, I have a dreamy memory of the priest's murmurings in Latin, the bride and groom, more of the incense, and the presence of something I could not name.

I went to bed early that night. I wanted to fall asleep, then wake up with the usual dread of another three hours of Sunday School and church service; and I wanted that sad ache to go away, or at least to know the source of it. Closing my eyes, I drifted toward sleep. Then, as though having fallen through some cosmic hole, I had the sensation of tumbling backwards in slow motion, and into some other place where I was surrounded by stars. The physical sensation of it was like the best part of being dizzy, as when my friends and I would twirl round and round, finally falling to the grass and watching the world spin.

Then: *Who am I?*

The voice was soft, intimate. But where had it come from? Was it my voice? That *presence* I'd sensed? Was the question about me? About *it*? I was more curious than frightened. The tumbling continued, and the question repeated every ten or fifteen seconds until I fell asleep.

Our after-church meal on that or any Sunday was pot roast, mashed potatoes, a canned green vegetable, pull-apart rolls browned in the oven, a lettuce and tomato salad with French dressing, and a world-class dessert—pecan or apple pie, or chocolate cake with ice cream, or brownies. I'd not eaten breakfast, and was still not hungry, but ate to satisfy my mother. My buddies wanted me to come out but I begged off, claiming too much homework, then closed myself in my room, lay down, and shut my eyes. The tumbling started, then the question, then sleep.

Sunday night was always leftovers followed by *Bonanza*. As soon as the lights were out and my eyes closed, the tumbling and the question returned. Then, after a few minutes: *Who am I asking the question? Who am I?*

The next few months were a time for baffled wonder. Something was different about me, but what? Moreover, what was the point? I was a twelve-year-old boy awash in the cultural zeitgeist of southeast Texas in the late 1950s, where boys were supposed to play football, learn to shoot things, and grow up to be like their daddies, where low-church Protestantism reigned supreme and it was not unusual to hear absurdist whisperings such as *Catholics don't even believe in Jesus; they think the pope is God*. So, exactly what was I supposed to do with a peculiar experience I'd had in, of all places, a Roman Catholic Church, one that wouldn't go away, and, depending on the day, was making me a little crazy? I wanted to talk to someone, but to whom? Almost certainly my nonreligious father would've half-listened, rolled his eyes, and said, *Go talk to your mother.* Who'd have listened, then dragged me down the street to the pastor's house; or called together church members for a full-throttle gang-save; or phoned my grandfather, who might well have boarded the next train with the intention of saving me from eternity in Hell.

I was pretty much on my own, with two boys inside my skin, one who wanted it all to go away, another who couldn't wait to turn out the lights, who hadn't a clue what was happening, but trusted it more than the other boy had ever trusted anything.

Besides, there *did* seem to be a certain logic in what was happening. Given that its genesis was in a church, it followed that I was having a "religious" experience, and that my attitude toward church would shift—certainly a result that would thrill my mother and grandparents. It shifted all right—to a track that would end in a sort of ontological train-wreck. Sunday School, worship services, and other church activities soon became like visits to an asylum in which nothing made sense. There were times when being there was so intolerable that I feared I might lose control and start screaming, though at what, or about what, I didn't know.

The tumbling and the questions repeated each night for months, then several times a week for the next few years. The questions were never intrusive, but more like koans, satisfied to *be* rather than demanding answers—a relief, since I had none. Finally, it all stopped. Then, almost ten years after it had started, it happened again—or seemed to—this time in an Episcopal church during the Nuptial Mass for my college roommate. Whether it was a repeat of the same event, anamnesis, or simple déjà vu, the tumbling and the questions returned, as did the sadness, which, finally, I recognized as hunger and longing.

Though it was a single moment, a split second in my sixty years, the man I've become, all that I've done in my professional life—parish priest (Episcopal), speaker and trainer for an international foundation, management consultant, writer—can be traced to it. And yet it remains a mystery. I've tried saying it was "of God," but the name arrives like a king and his court; there is simply too much baggage and too many extras for my small house. Other names present the same. I've come to prefer the mystery, the illogicalness in the fact that I understand it far better when I don't try to understand it.

Understanding has its own timetable and comes when I'm not looking for it. While still a teenager, the word "milieu" came as a welcome guest because that was the sense of it for me that Saturday afternoon—an immersion, a surrounding too vast ever to say, "It's here, but not there" or "under this roof, but not that one." Later I would stumble across the Latin, *Mysterium Tremendum*, and know the meaning without asking, and the vast experience to which it pointed. Some years back, I came across the German mystic Meister Eckhart, who centuries ago wrote, "That which one says is God, he is not; that which one does not say, he is more truly that than that which one says he is." Except for the "G" word and the gendering, it fit for me, sort of. I've loved the image inherent there, of the definition of the infinite existing only in the spaces between the words, whether written or spoken. There has been no form, no pillar of fire or burning bush. Moreover, there's been nothing to believe in. In fact, I've come to think that trying to believe in what happened that day is the worst idea of all.

John Coats is a minister in Texas.

When I Knew
Godlessness and God on September 11

Patrick Giles

It wasn't when the first tower fell, or when I could hear—on the phone with a friend who lived very close—the second tower come clattering down.

It wasn't when I stood at 9th Avenue and 14th Street to catch my breath, and by turning my head just an inch to the right saw serene people safe in the beautiful light and air, and then by turning my head just an inch to the left saw a sky blackening with dust from the two buildings, and right before me silent tangles of people covered by the detritus of coworkers and friends numbly trying to find their way home.

It wasn't when I managed to get within a few blocks of where those buildings had been, buildings I'd worked in, and I was stopped by a young cop, who answered my hoarse *don't you understand? There are thousands of people down there!* With his *Mister, I just saw, and there's nobody down there,* that I felt my soul roll its eyes to find the grace of God.

But there was no sign of Him anywhere.

All those moments reminded me of others: the moment when a concentration camp survivor described to me what it was like to survive mass murder, to keep going when the smoke of that day's dead palled the entire camp and made breathing impossible; or the day during my AIDS volunteering when four people with AIDS I had cared for died within a few hours of each other, on the same floor of the same hospital, and even the nurses were scrambling from terror, the empty hospital hallway full of the sounds of sobbing and slamming doors.

But that moment, on the street in New York on September 11, at that moment I felt again what I had on those earlier days, I felt what I dreaded above everything else, even death itself: at that moment I believed in Godlessness.

So, no, He never reached down to take my arm or lend me his shoulder. The clouds refused to part. His voice wasn't rolling anywhere, even amid squealing of collapsing girders and shrieks of exploding glass that could be heard from more than a mile away, or among the people getting bottled water for wanderers on the street, some of them so blanketed by ash they looked scorched, or among the people who didn't make it downtown running into a neighbor or colleague who did, the neighbor or colleague raising his voice to say Don't you understand? Hardly anybody got out, I don't know how I made it, the others were all still up there, or among the people camped out hopefully on stoops of friends' or lovers' houses eager for a reunion.

But something did happen later, downtown, just before twilight, when I was standing a half mile away from It, with hundreds of other people eager to help somebody, anybody. A young women whose face was still grayed by layers of ash stammered she had stood before the tower she'd worked in (trying not to be thankful a long line at the coffee shop had kept her outside) and forced herself to pray for each person she saw falling—I asked God to turn them into angels right away, before . . . and she paused, her sweet voice answered by a roar that maybe we both thought was some kind of attempt at an answer, even though it made the air itself cringe. Everybody turned heads south to see 7 or 11 WTC collapsing, and another giant cloud of debris swallowing block after block in seconds, hot on our trail. I remember the sound of hundreds of feet pounding north in an instant, of rushing and rushing forward as hard as I could, even though I held no hope anymore and as the first whoosh of hot pursuing air pushed forward on the asphalt to slow down our feet I found myself not minding that this might be the last feeling I'd ever know.

It still wasn't exactly then, either. It really began a moment later, when a hand grabbed my left arm and pulled (I was one of the slowest people in the crowd), and other people pulled slower ones along with them as they ran, and a voice like out of another older Fall trembled as it cried Don't look back!, and another hand reached amid the whirl of breaths and foot-beats towards mine to help me along, and a crunching, sucking sound shoved every other sound out of the way as I saw in windows of buildings alongside me the cloud getting nearer and nearer, but we kept running, and it stopped following us.

My lungs had given up the ghost, and as I searched for a sewer to stick my face into (someone else had done this when the first tower fell, and had told me about it) I tried not to look back, and muttered to hell with Lot's wife, and I turned to look back. The debris cloud was half a block away, hovering enormous and splendid and so full of the power of suffering I almost bowed before it; but just short of crossing the street it had paused, as if having consumed so much that was human it had learned politeness and was waiting for the traffic light to change (I could see around its edges two little red lights winking to green) before it came after us afresh. Or maybe, as the cloud just stayed where it was, it seemed as if some force bigger than evil had put a hand on the thing, made it pile upon itself up and up into the sky (as it was now doing, its ascending rumbles as shocking as enraged curses) rather than gallop forward to engulf us, because whatever had suddenly exercised restraint over it had spent the day watching thousands die and millions despair and had finally tossed omnipotence, forced a gap between more death and us, as if quietly but firmly saying to everything, enough.

That's when I thought at the time, amid the sound of hundreds of lungs wheezing with relief, and loud plops as bodies fell only a few feet to the gutter, not dead but crying and very alive. We weren't alone; we weren't abandoned; we weren't worthless and graceless; something or someone had stepped in and saved us; we could still live. Thank God, thank God, I heard a hundred times in ten seconds from inches or blocks away. But, I thought, a moment before I could thank God myself, and get up and start walking home again, Why can't I, even after a moment like this, ever be certain I really have anyone to thank?

Patrick Giles was a writer in New York; he died in 2007.

THE LATE MISTER BIN LADEN:
A NOTE

BRIAN DOYLE

And what could anyone add to the ocean of comment and opinion and conclusion and musing and snarling and vengeful remarks published and shouted about the recent death of Mr. O. bin Laden, late of Abbottabad, Pakistan, shot to death in his bedroom, perhaps with his television remote in his hand, perhaps moments after he finished coloring his beard black again for a video production scheduled for the morning? Not much, especially in my case, after nearly ten years of quiet rage that he murdered three of my friends on September 11, cackling over their deaths, a cackle I will never forget as long as I live. And yet, and yet, I find myself thinking how very sad; not his death, in which the bullets he had so often assigned to others found him at last, but his life, wasted on a foolish and murderous idea, causing such epic wreckage, and perhaps in the end doing far more damage to his beloved religion than anyone else in its long and often admirable history.

I say this as a Catholic man, well aware that my religion tried bin Laden's idea, and found it a roaring failure, responsible for uncountable deaths of innocent souls; we call our collective campaign of savagery the Crusades, and even the most rabid among Catholics today cannot say with a straight face that our attacks on the infidel succeeded in anything except gaining the Church a well-deserved reputation for militant murder; and from those bloody years the Church sensibly retreated back mostly to a business model, spending the next seven hundred years as one of the largest, richest, most influential, riveting, and troubled corporations in human history. Entrepreneurial Catholic individuals murdered and robbed the pagans of the New World, certainly, but as a religion, rather than murder other established religions we sought to outpopulate them, ignore them, negotiate complex truces, or, as we did recently with the Anglicans, offer them readmission to the mother ship from which years ago they disembarked, in their case because of the sexual politics of kings, one of the great human spectator sports. In a real sense, after the Crusades finally petered to their ignominious end, we matured as a religion, we realized that the sword was the worst of persuasive devices, and we turned to other hinges of history, some brilliant, like the public relations geniuses Mother Teresa of India, Karol Wojtyła of Poland, Dorothy Day of Brooklyn, and the elementary school system on which much of modern Catholicism was built. Today, long centuries after we waged holy war against people who called God other names than we did, there are a billion Catholics in the world, and two billion followers of the devout Jew Yeshuah ben Joseph.

It was the fervent dream of the late Mr. bin Laden that an epic war arise between the nearly two billion followers of Muhammad ibn 'Abdullah, blessed be his name, and the followers of Yeshuah ben Joseph, blessed be his name, and this fiery dream, born in 1998 with the murder of Kenyan and Tanzanian innocents, consumed twenty years of what must have been a very bright intellect, an often-attested-to personal charisma, and a mountainous personal fortune, and again I find myself thinking how sad this was, how misguided, how twisted. What a waste of gifts given to that man by the Creator! Imagine, for a moment, the same man alert to humor, perhaps the greatest weapon of all. Imagine the same man, humorless in this life, infused by the holy merriment of a John XXIII, a Dalai Lama, a Desmond Tutu. Imagine that same poor soul, consumed day and night by smoldering hate and worries about rehearsing his lines for his video performances, alert to the power of mercy, apology, simplicity, conversation, common ground. Imagine what he might have done for the religion he loved, had he bent his capacious talents to witty connection rather than wanton destruction. Imagine, for a moment, that he might have become a great man, rather than the preening thug he was, wrapped in a shawl, obsessed with himself, hiding in a dark room, waiting for the explosive death he must have known would someday be his fate. What a waste.

Brian Doyle is the editor of Portland Magazine, *and the author of* Grace Notes, *a collection of essays, from ACTA Publications in Chicago.*

BALD PLACES

Notes on nursing as witness.

HOB OSTERLUND

ROOMS 652 AND 653 couldn't be more different, except they're both bald.

Room 652 is a woman with a glioblastoma. It's the kind of brain tumor that often kills fast, usually within six months of diagnosis. She's 57. Her name is Teea. The doctor says I'm history, says Teea softly, without apparent fear. Her humor is deceptive. I bet she'd bribe, threaten, or supplicate all creatures, medical or otherwise, two-legged or four, who promised they could buy her even one extra week. She wants to live so bad she could scream it to the heavenly rafters, but she doesn't, at least not in the hospital. She behaves calmly here.

Each of her three daughters is as beautiful as their mama, even though radiation therapy fried the hair right off their mama's head. She only has curly clumps above her ears now, like a clown. I'm thinking of having them bronzed, she says, so she can put the last follicular evidence from the upper end of her body on her mantle above the fireplace, next to her baby boots. Nobody remarks that the boots are from the beginning of her life and the hair is likely to be from the end of it.

The oldest daughter is studying primates somewhere in Africa, and came home two days after her grandmother telephoned. The middle daughter's in the air force, is training to be a pilot. The youngest lives nearby, her dancer's body temporarily compromised by an unexpected pregnancy offered as a good-bye gift from a yoga instructor. All three are with their mother in the hospital as regular as rain.

Teea figures the lion's share of her own parenting duties are behind her, and she wants to sit back on some padded chaise lounge, drink a nice Australian wine, and watch her daughters do what they do best. She wants to be the audience. Applaud, witness, detach if she can, but not die.

Room 653 is bald too, clean-shaven after smashing into a windshield of a stolen car he careened into oncoming traffic. Both the men he hit died right there on the highway—a father driving his visiting son to the airport, a young and popular volleyball player, finishing his college career with 731 digs. His grinning picture was all over the news.

Even though the wreck was mid-afternoon, 653's blood toxicology screen was positive for methamphetamines, benzodiazepines, alcohol, and cocaine.

He's skinny. Street drugs suppressed his appetite's voice, tricking him into thinking he was not just high, but full. At first glance his body looks like it belongs to an emaciated, dying old man. Closer up it's easy to see his sculpted muscles are like hardwood. He's seventeen years old. He wears a plastic diaper, and his limbs are splayed like a book, his feet and hands tied to each corner of the bed so he doesn't hurt himself or us nurses. He yells nearly constantly. Most of the noises are unintelligible, but he does seem to know three words: *sit, no, how.* We're suspicious that sit is a mispronunciation. More often than not, how is a long sound with several syllables, like a chant. The emphasis is usually on the ow, leading us to wonder if he's in pain. We nurses give him analgesics even though the meds don't seem to do much. We give the meds because it makes us feel like we're doing something useful. We give them because his yelling drives us crazy.

He's a hard one to like, is 653. Most of the time all we can do is re-tie him, put mitts on his hands so he doesn't chew into his own fingers or scratch himself bloody, clean him up from time to time. I've never seen anyone visit him, but there's a note on his board that says *Grandma and Noni love you. Get well soon.*

For someone tethered in four places, 653 is all over the bed. In just two weeks he's already rubbed his heels down to the bone. His diaper hangs low on his angled hips, and most of the time he's able to squirm out of it. If he gets his hands loose he tears up the diaper and eats it. Or throws punches. Last week he gave a night shift nurse a nasty bruise on her upper arm while she was pushing a syringe of liquid food into a gastric tube going into his abdomen. While her focus was on his G-tube, he bit through the wrist restraint and swung at an enemy none of the rest of us can see.

Teea is my age, and we've had a few good talks about God and destiny and health. Today, however, I spend my precious few extra moments here with 653. I don't really want to, but my job (as a pain and palliative care clinical nurse specialist) is to assess his discomfort. I also want to relieve the pain of the staff nurses, which will happen briefly if I can quiet him down.

His name is Brandon. I discovered yesterday that if I call him by name, he stops yelling. But when I start to leave he just starts up again, no matter how many tranquilizers or opiates the nurses give him.

"Brandon!" I shout over his shout. He makes full-on eye contact and stares like a baby does, not quite in focus but very intent on something he sees. Does he recognize his own name long enough to stop the spinning of some kaleidoscope of fears that dominate his visual field?

"Brandon, do you have pain?"

"No," he says, as clearly as if we'd just resumed a lucid conversation over a cup of coffee.

I take a couple of charts into his room. After I say his name and he goes silent, I do some paperwork. He stares at me, he stares at the walls, he stares into thin air. Every once in a while he tracks something across the ceiling, as if a shooting star has flared above him. His temporary quiet is a relief.

I tell him about things. Tonight I tell him I want to make a movie of him, to show high school kids what really happens on drugs. I figure the diaper might get them. I ask him how could it be that some people want to live with every fiber of their spirit, and others seem to dare death to come get them. Brandon doesn't argue or interrupt. He lies there in total silence. He doesn't do it because he hears just any words, but because he hears a voice speak his name. His name is his talisman, his clue, his Geiger counter, his compass, his home base, his organizer, his horizon, his divining rod.

"Brandon, I have to go." He stares at my lips as if he hears something remotely familiar and unnerving, like the pulsing of a troubled mother's heart.

Heading toward Teea's room, I see her husband, Robbie, leaning against the wall outside her door. His eyes greet me with a grief as dense as the door itself, and a question that has no answer. Still, his grief is soft somehow, a metal tempered with gratitude. Grief tempered by guilt is barbed wire.

I lean up against the wall next to him. He tells me that the hardest thing about Teea's diagnosis is the helplessness. A high school biology teacher, he likes tangibles. He tells me the ground beneath his feet moves like sand, he cannot find purchase.

Noooooooooooooo, shouts Brandon from 653.

I follow Robbie into Teea's room.

Honey, says Teea, seeing her husband's helplessness. *Go sit with that young man next door*, and Robbie leaves willingly, taking his question with him.

Hob Osterlund is a writer, nurse, and scholar of humor as nursing tool. She is the author of the remarkable book Holy Mōlī: Albatross and Other Ancesters, *about albatrosses and holiness.*

GOD OWNS A CONVENIENCE STORE IN BRITISH COLUMBIA

Who knew?

GAE RUSK

GOD OWNS A CONVENIENCE STORE in the city of Vancouver, in Canada. His store is on Broadway, not far from the University, and God sells everything there, lottery tickets, pastries, beer, paper towels, but what I need is cash, so I park and go in to use the store's convenient money machine, from which I happily buy two hundred Canadian dollars.

In this incarnation, God made himself into a man from North India, running a small business in Canada. This time, God made me into a woman from Oklahoma, raised in New Mexico.

I look up from the money machine and see God standing behind the counter watching me.

After counting my new cash, I am impelled to buy something to legitimize my use of the money machine, but what? Not fruit pies. Not fancy air fresheners, not arthritis-repelling bracelets, but what? I circle the aisles, passing cases of chilled beverages and racks of salted chips. Then I find a candy display bulwarking the cash register at the heart of the store. I love candy, and I love that God sells candy, and I am thinking this very thought when I spy pink grapefruit Mentos.

I first heard about this new flavor from another Mento junkie who bought a roll in Tokyo, and I have suffered Mento envy ever since. Now, glory be to God, here are pink grapefruit Mentos for sale in His crowded convenience store on Broadway.

I pull out twenty dollars, still warm from the money machine, to pay for four rolls of Mentos. I want all the rolls, all thirty or more, but I cannot practice such greed right in front of God, nor can I lie and claim the candy is for my son's soccer team, so I plunk down the money next to those mere four rolls of Mentos, and it is at this moment that God grabs my hand and studies my rings.

They are reddish-purple stars, either rubies or sapphires, depending on the light and whom you believe. One is set in gold, I had it made in Katmandu many years ago, and my older daughter gave me the other one, the one set in silver. I wear both rings twined together to remind me that I am wed to my children and wed to myself, and it is up to me to make it all work for everyone.

God brushes the Mentos aside and touches my wrist. I worry the candy will roll away, but it doesn't budge and instead sits there sparkling and humming. God studies my two rings. He peers into my palm. He asks my birth date. God forgot my birthday? He must be getting old, too.

God's hands are rough and dry, the hands of someone who works for a living. They are perfectly warm. They vibrate. His eyes are mirrors of mica and mercury. His eyes compel me to listen. They adjure me to remember what He says as He reads my palms like the lyrics of two hymns in a key I have never before heard.

When God works out my numerology on a sales slip, the results make him smile. He tells me many true things right there at the checkout counter, then he works the numbers for my three kids, for my parents, for my ex-husband, even for my first boyfriend, and I am transfixed by it all.

When I have to leave, God leans forward and tells me I have a big angel living in my heart. Huge, he says. Enormous. According to God, at least half my heart is filled with this lively angel, who irradiates my blood and drives my deeds and generally lights the runway of life for me, and for anyone else who lands nearby.

God finally releases my hands. I look at them to see if the pulsing sensation is visible. My hands look normal, except the two rubies are strobing brilliant stars. God blesses me as I stumble off, my stunned hands clutching four rolls of Mentos in the prayer position. God warns me to drive more carefully. He says he has noticed my tendency to be other-minded, and I marvel again that He knows me so well.

Then I drive more erratically than ever, because my angel is wide-awake and throbbing in my chest, my rings are blinding the oncoming traffic, and it is hard to hold the wheel with my hands still needling back to normal.

Gae Rusk is a writer in Hawaii. For more of her work see gaerusk.com.

THE REALITY OF TORTURE

MARTIN FLANAGAN

TORTURE—TO ME, THE MOST REPUGNANT of all human practices—is coming back into intellectual fashion. I realized this recently when I saw an advertisement for an Oxford University Press book bringing together "an array of social experts to debate the advisability and implications of maintaining the absolute ban on torture."

Next to that ad was one for a book on dance music from the 1940s. Above it was an ad for a history of Latin as a language. And there was the Oxford ad, utilizing a tone of high reason and invoking the authority of social experts, for a book admitting the possibility that torture was okay.

That advertisement would not have appeared five years ago. Something's changed. The something is us.

If I state clearly what I mean in this essay at some point I will be called irrational. If I go on about it long enough, I may well be called other things as well. Persistent anti-slavery campaigners in the United States prior to the Civil War were termed "morbid." In a lifetime of going to church, Mark Twain's mother never heard slavery once attacked from the pulpit. Lincoln summarized the absurdity of the legislative position when he said that Northerners didn't talk about slavery in their legislature because it wasn't their business and they didn't talk about it on their visits to the Southern legislature because it wasn't their place.

The so-called super-realists among us will say that torture has ever been among us and ever will be. Perhaps. And there may be nothing I can do about that. But I do have some small say in what passes for civilized discourse. Never in my adult life have I felt my understanding of that term collapse beneath me as it did than when I came across the advertisement for a book on torture.

Like so much in our changed world, the return of torture into intellectual fashion dates back to September 11, from which arose, among much else, the "ticking bomb" argument: A terror suspect has set a bomb which is about to go off. Unless you find out where, innocents will be killed and injured. Is torturing the suspect wrong?

This is a tabloid argument. It reduces the murky swirling morality of places like Abu Ghraib to one enormously simple and attractive proposition. I don't believe torture is that simple. For example, what if the suspect refuses to speak? Is it permissible, as happens in some countries, to torture a member of the suspect's family in front of them? If western democracies abandon what the *Economist* magazine has called their "taboo" on torture, where exactly does the new limit to behavior lie? And why?

I also have a continuing problem with the word *terrorist*. I am not denying the presence of people in the world so consumed by their mission to destroy that they will harm others without thought of human consequence. But this debate demands far greater precision since the word *terrorist* is now commonly used to mean anyone who takes up arms against a state, regardless of political causes.

I will explain myself by outlining the case of a largely forgotten man exiled to these shores from his native land in 1849 after leading an armed uprising against the great imperial power of the day. I regard this man, William Smith O'Brien, as the champion of my people, the starving poor of Ireland, a million of whom died during these years or emigrated or, like my forebear, stole to feed their families and were transported as convicts to Tasmania.

O'Brien was not a violent radical. Educated at Harrow and Cambridge, he was a unique expression of the old European aristocratic culture. He was fond of Queen Victoria. But he also stood in direct descent from the last king of Ireland and was highly mindful of the fact. For twenty years, he had been a conscientious member of the House of Commons, applying himself to issues ranging from the transportation of convicts to slavery, which he steadfastly opposed.

He sought to address the problems of Ireland through the imperial parliament while seeking to counter the violent tendencies in the nationalist movement back in Ireland. Time and again, he rose in the house to ask questions of government policy. He demanded the Irish famine be treated as a national calamity like war and bitterly attacked the English government's habit of addressing the horror in terms of laissez-faire economic theory.

Eventually, faced with scenes of mass suffering in Ireland and despairing of parliament, he sought help from the government of France—in the popular imagination of the day, England's enemy. When he returned, he said he would not take up arms to free Ireland but he would defend existing rights. Further rights were taken away. The uprising he led was short-lived and futile. O'Brien was sentenced to be hanged, drawn, and quartered, the sentence being commuted to exile to Australia.

O'Brien's story shows how a decent man can become embroiled in political violence. His captivity was structured so that no one spoke to him but an official. His diaries record his losing battle to keep his mind from turning inward. He believed he was being tortured—though his experience on Maria Island in 1849 was a holiday camp compared with the other convicts there and with what we now know about Guantanamo Bay and the prisons of Iraq.

I have a friend, a black South African, who was tortured in Zimbabwe by Robert Mugabe's paranoid regime. I will call my friend Stephen. He is as good a man as I have met, humble and true. He told me that after three months of being tortured he no longer knew what he believed. He told me two men "worked" on him. One apologized and said he was doing it because he had no choice, the other didn't apologize at all. Maybe Stephen was his idea of a ticking bomb. I didn't ask Stephen what had been done to him but briefly, in his eyes, I saw a wild liquid fear that reflected the horrible injury done to him in every way.

Before meeting Stephen I had gone to Robbin Island where Nelson Mandela was detained. The man who showed us around had been tortured and was scarcely sane. We entered the dormitory where he had been locked up each night and he flung shut the metal door so that it clanged mightily in our ears. Most of us were looking the other way and jumped. "That is how they shut it," he cried. Painted in ghostly writing on the brick wall at the other end of the dormitory were the words Happy Days Are Here Again.

Our guide gave us a full account of his torture. His limbs had been bound to his body with chains, then he had been lifted to a height of five feet and dropped on to a cement floor. Lifted and dropped, lifted and dropped. His hands had been tied behind his back. An Alsatian had savaged his genitals. Having told us this and more, he marched off, throwing his hands about and talking loudly. He broke into tears when saying goodbye.

It was after telling us of his torture that we swept past Mandela's cell. Of a size a prize animal might be kept in at a rural show, it was completely open to view. No privacy. It was from this bare place, surrounded by damaged people like our guide, that Mandela not only converted the other prisoners of his belief in human dignity but also some of his guards.

Stephen took me to his home. He had two small boys, about six and three, who had just been caught up in the excitement of the cricket World Cup. We played backyard cricket. Stephen came out and played too. So there we were in the late golden glow of an African day, a smell of dust in the air. As an Australian male born after World War II, what greater image of boyhood innocence could I possess than a game of backyard cricket? But the man with whom I was playing this innocent game had been tortured. This wasn't an issue of race. His torturers, like him, were black. The moral relativities of the 20th century couldn't find a way around this one. That day I knew I could no longer deny the existence of evil.

I don't claim to be a wholly rational man, but who is? Anyone who says they can be detached about a subject like torture is fatally disconnected from what the great poet of the First World War trenches, Wilfred Owen, called "the eternal reciprocity of tears." Wilfred Owen considered such people cursed.

The arguments for torture, like so many of the arguments for war, are always presented as the work of super-realists—the sort who come to the fore in times of crisis when all illusions of human existence are swept away—but you would have to be naïve or worse to believe torture can be conducted, as is now being argued, under controlled circumstances. As I understand it, the Inquisition was also conducted under controlled circumstances; the inquisitors were not allowed to draw blood, just break bones and pull limbs from sockets.

Torture is evil. Sanction the practice and it will assume the character of an institution with those who do it best rising to positions of command.

In writing this essay I have tried to explain my beliefs in a personal way. I challenge those arguing for torture, in whatever form or circumstance, to do the same. Take us behind the walls of your proclamations. Show us who you really are. What makes you believe as you do? I challenge those people to put their opinions to one side, and tell us a story about the reality of torture. Here's mine.

When I left South Africa, Stephen ran me to the airport. We had become close and talked a lot. Stephen had turned back from the use of violence as a political weapon during the apartheid years, having seen where it led. Instead he worked for peace. It was at the airport that he told me those few details of his torture.

We were standing at a desk awaiting service. I'd lost my ticket. All I had to get back to Australia was a name on a piece of paper. South Africa is part first world, part third world, and you're never sure which part you're getting. The man with the piece of paper had been gone ten minutes when he reappeared in the distance. I was going to run over and grab him. Stephen looked at him and me and said, Trust him. It usually works.

It did. Stephen, a small man, is a moral mountain. I choose to be guided by him, and people like him.

As unimaginable as it may now seem, the issue of torture goes way beyond our time. The war against terror began as a moral crusade, a war against evil. Now our man-made moral universe is being reshaped, and with phenomenal speed. I am reminded of the words of the great Aboriginal leader Patrick Dodson, who said to me recently that he thought we were on the edge of a new Dark Age.

The arguments for torture haven't really changed since the Inquisition. What has changed is what's terrifying us and who we suspect its agents among us to be. What has changed is us.

Martin Flanagan, one of Australia's finest writers, is the author of the remarkable The Game in Time of War, *among many other books.*

A BURNING SOUL

MARY GORDON

THE DAY OF MY FIRST COMMUNION was a perfect day. May 19, 1956: the single date I can call up with the assurance that it marks a time in which I was completely happy. On that day I had no doubt that I had mastered everything that was required of me. The rest was in the hands of people whose competence, or more properly, expertise, was beyond question. This would never happen in my life again.

The preparations for the great event extended from mid-winter to the height of spring. From the beginning of February to the 18th of May, when each one of us would make his or her First Confession, a large part of each school day was devoted to making us ready to receive the sacrament. And from that time, the first grade classroom, which had been for me a locus of plain dread, became transformed.

My dread had started with my first step over the threshold, when I entered the room, pulled from my father in a flood of tears (he may have wept as well). I was oppressed, as if my shoes were perpetually wet, by the classroom's smells: sour milk, bologna sandwiches steeping, simmering, in tin lunch boxes in the cloakroom whose doors did not provide sufficient barriers to keep the odors from me. And, except for catechism, whose precision I enjoyed, I was bored by the curriculum. I already knew how to read and write; pretending I was on a level with the others enervated me and gave me my first deep lessons in contempt; drawing and mathematics seemed to me ridiculous, beside what I knew to be the point of everything: words.

And there were requirements for a kind of orderliness I considered both unimportant and entirely beyond me. Folding your paper in four to make identical columns separated from each other by a nearly invisible crease. Covering books in brown paper. Keeping books in a particular order in the desk. Other protocols, which did not involve my controlling objects in the physical world, objects that had clearly vowed to fox and vex me, I quite liked. I was very good at sitting in silence with my hands folded perfectly in front of me on the top of the desk. But hanging my hat exactly right on the hook reserved for me in the back cloakroom: this I could not do.

Some time in the month of October, I vomited in class, ruining my penmanship book, whose cover, green with black Palmer method letter spelling out "Penmanship," had to be ripped off by Sister Trinitas, who dealt with everything calmly, efficiently, and made me feel, remarkably, no shame. She was a lovely woman, a kind woman, a calm woman, beautifully contained, sheathed, but what the sheath enclosed was not a sword, rather a lily, odorless, white, formal; she seemed quite as much a symbol as a living thing. Her skin was very white, waxen almost, like the texture of a beeswax candle. Her paleness seemed almost sacramental because when you thought of her your mind immediately went to things that in themselves touched on the sacred: blessed candles, Easter lilies, and she was hidden, precious, like the host concealed in the darkness of the tabernacle, whose interior none of the likes of us would ever see.

After I vomited, she took me down to the nurse's office, and while I looked at the posters of the five basic food groups and allowed my eye to fall on the machine to test our hearing, she and the nurse agreed that I should be sent home. The uncalled-for holiday changed everything. After that, my dread diminished incrementally but irregularly, throughout the fall and early winter. I don't know why: perhaps it was the surprise, almost a shock, that what I had imagined would be an occasion for shaming became a moment of gracious care. But it took the furnace of preparations of my First Communion to transform the room into a place of purpose, where everything, in its clear importance, in its obvious essentialness, became delightful. The room turned from the center of dark banishment to a place of light: high windows opened by a pole with a hook at the end which only Sister Trinitas could reach, the rest of us being much too small.

Everything I was listening to seemed wholly desirable. There was so much to be learned. It was the kind of learning that had the surplus value of teaching me, or allowing me to know, that I did not need my parents. I could get along without them. I did not need anyone: I belonged to God.

There were fifty of us packed into that room in those crowded postwar days. Triumphalist times: Catholic children not sent to Catholic schools risked their immortal souls through contamination, the mere potential of being put in danger by careless parents, sent to public school, into the mixed, non-Catholic world, as if they'd been frivolously sent into the plague ward for convenience, because the quarantine was too much trouble, too expensive, too much work.

And so we sat, half a hundred of us, in the weak light of late winter, early spring, our hands folded on the maple desktops where some wicked child may have carved his name, a desktop we would each polish with a half lemon given to each child on the last day of class, one of the last days of June: but that warmth, that release, was in the future. Now it was March, April, and the light was silvery, still, with a hint of ice menacing it, and we sat, expectant, even in the most disobedient attentive.

There were catechism questions to be memorized, but we had done that sort of thing before: Who is God, God is the Supreme Being, Why did God make me, to know him, to love him and to serve him in this world and to be happy with him forever in heaven. So the definitions of the Eucharist—The Eucharist is the body and blood of Christ in the form of bread and wine—were simply an extension of something we had already learned before.

But in addition to the catechism questions, we had to memorize a special prayer, longer than any we had yet learned. Far longer than the Our Father. We were not yet judged ready for the Apostles Creed, although my family, ambitious for my spiritual distinction, had taught it to me. This new prayer we would say in the darkness made by the screen of our hands in front of our closed eyes. We would say it in silence, part of what was called "making a Thanksgiving." But now, to learn it, we said it aloud, fifty of us crying out with one voice:

Look down upon me good and gentle Jesus while before thy face I humbly kneel and with burning soul pray and beseech thee to fix deep within my heart lively sentiments of faith, hope and charity, true contrition for my sins and a firm purpose of amendment. While I contemplate, with great love and tender pity, the words which David thy prophet said of thee my Jesus: "They have pierced my hands and my feet. They have numbered all my bones."

Never had any words pleased me so much. I would not have put it this way then, but I know now: it was the mix of the physical, the metaphysical, and the historical in this prayer that struck a chord of ultimate rightness, ultimate satisfactoriness, of many tones being hit straight on and with full resonance. I have never known who wrote these words, and from what historical period they arose.

You will say it is ridiculous to assume that six- and seven-year-olds could have any understanding of these words. But it is not ridiculous. I knew what a burning soul was: I was an ardent girl, any experience of ardor I have had since then is only a re-capitulation, a diluted version of what I felt as a child. It was easy for me to believe that my soul was burning because I had a clear image of what my soul might be. It was an oval, the shape that Sister Trinitas had traced with a white chalk line on the board, then filled in with splotches made of red chalk, representing sin, which could be erased—poof, like that—by the sacrament of penance, represented by the eraser. But no, my soul was not a simple oval, it was flame shaped, the flame I could fix with my eye at the top of the candle, and I could feel it burning within me, my desire to love God, to be good, to be good not for the sake of other human beings, and not even for the fear of hell fire, but because not to be good, to sin, would be to betray the love of God, who had died for me. And so I did feel great love; I did feel tender pity: Jesus had suffered unto death on the cross for me, he would have done it if I had been the only person in the world. I knew that as well as I knew the words to the Pledge of Allegiance and that I was an American child, and that the communists would kill me for being both Catholic and American if they got a chance.

Most thrilling to me were the parts of the prayer that began with "While I call to mind the word which David thy prophet said of thee my Jesus: 'they have pierced my hands and my feet; they have numbered all my bones.'" My father's name was David, and I knew I was half Jewish, so to hear the name David was to have my heritage invoked and to underscore what I suspected; my lineage was more ancient, more burnished, deeper-rooted than any of my classmates. And I could feel in my body the words *pierce* and *number*, they made my flesh thrum; I could imagine the nails going straight through the tender flesh in the top of my arch. In the shoe stores that sold Buster Brown shoes (the boy, the dog on the inner sole, stepped on every morning brutally by children all over America), you could put your foot in an X-ray machine and see each one of your small bones. I brought this image to mind when I thought of the Roman soldiers, crushing bone after bone, ripping my feet, then when they got to my hands, puncturing then drilling through the tender spot below my knuckles, still dimpled, still babyish, nevertheless able to mimic the pain of the crucified Lord.

With this knowledge, the words I had absorbed into my skin made my body no longer an encumbrance, an irrelevance, but part of the sacrament, a necessary vessel, sacred in itself: My body would contain the host, it would house the body of Christ. In the presence of the host, which we would take inside our mouth and swallow, as we might swallow ordinary food (but everything about this was extraordinary), He would become our guest. We sang this as an idea contained in the hymn we all learned, sitting still in our wooden desks with their empty ink-wells (first graders were allowed pencils only) in our stiff serge navy blue uniforms (jumpers and white Dacron blouses for girls, long pants, Dacron shirts, blue clip-on ties for boys), the equality of the ugliness a false promise of future equality, spread out on a larger terrain.

Sister Trinitas would put the silver pitch pipe between her calm lips, and her beautiful white cheeks would swell like a Botticelli Zephyr's as she blew the note and we prepared (each of our hearts in our mouths, and yet these hearts were high) to learn the hymn. It was called "Little White Guest," and we would sing it one day only, only one in our whole lives: the day of our First Communion.

We practiced the words many, many times. Hundreds of times it must have been, so I will never forget them. In a way that I cannot with any lines of great English poetry, I can call them to mind in a second:

You have come to my heart dearest Jesus
I'm holding you close to my breast
I am whispering over and over
You are welcome O Little White Guest
And now that you've come dearest Jesus
To nestle so close to my breast
I whisper I love you my Jesus
You are welcome O little White Guest.

This is the first time in my life that these words are a part of written rather than sung language. And as I type them and then read them, I see that they are entirely unremarkable: not an outstanding image, not a luminous word. Except for the central conceit: the little white guest. What could be more sentimental? But even now it strikes me, not as sentimental, but as poignant. At the time, although I was one of the children singing the hymn, I was aware of the poignancy of the image of children singing: I was simultaneously singing my heart out and swimming through a reflexive, rushing ocean of self-love.

One of the most important things to be drilled into our heads, and one of the greatest causes of anxiety, was the pre-Communion fast. In those pre–Vatican II days, one was required to fast from midnight of the night before taking the sacrament. I would, of course, be asleep for most of that time, but I had to be very careful, very very careful, vigilant to the point of death, not to pop something into my mouth on my way past the kitchen to the bathroom. I worried that even brushing my teeth might be a violation of the terms of the fast, but Sister Trinitas assured me it was not, when I raised my hand to ask the question. Did my classmates feel relief that I had voiced an anxiety they might have shared, or did they think I was a freak, ridiculous in my over-scrupulosity?

I knew that the emptiness I would feel that day would be a sacred emptiness, unlike any kind of ordinary hunger. I longed for it; but I feared—I had been warned so often—of the stupidity of my own flesh, its coarseness, its vulnerability to the temptations of the devil. To break the fast would not be sinful, but nonetheless would make the taking of the sacrament impossible. And, like little soldiers, we repeated the command, "Nothing must pass the lips after midnight." The repetition was meant to fix the idea, not only in our brain, but as if we had inscribed it, like M. in Kafka's penal colony, onto our flesh, the writing and rewriting, the inscription and re-inscription. Nothing after midnight. Nothing past the lips.

The day arrived: May 18th, the day of our First Confession, a day not of light but of darkness, the day of reckoning, one of the Dies Irae, where we must acknowledge our sinfulness, where the red blotches that had marred the souls left perfected at Baptism would be removed.

What were they thinking of? We were six, seven years old? How could we have sinned?

I was accused of a special sin, but by one accuser only: my mother (from my father, in all our time together, there was not one word of accusation, only the balm of absolute approbation, absolute love). My sin was touching the part of my body that was forbidden, and worse, the inability not to touch it when I had been told that touching it was vile, so vile that it must be kept secret from all the world.

And my mother told me, explicitly, that this was my special sin and that before communion it must be confessed.

I knew that no other child in the church that day had a vileness anywhere approaching mine. This weighed me down—but was I conscious of a kind of Counter-Reformation glamour: the sinner/penitent, penitence possible only because of sin, the old journey to the depths, finished now because I had climbed out of the pit and seen the crucifix: a point on which I could fix my eyes to give me courage to struggle out of the mire of loathsomeness to which my touching had consigned me? But no, that is a wishful looking back. I did not feel glamorous; I felt bad. But I was not a bad child. I was a very good child. All of us were. We were six years old.

How can we forgive them, why should we forgive them, for teaching us to say, when we had barely learned our ABCs, "Bless me Father for I have sinned . . ."?

The fifty of us were broken up into four lines, one for each confessional. Each confessional had two doors, or velvet curtains, through which the penitent walked, kneeling then in darkness on a hard wooden kneeler, apprehending, but not seeing the screen behind which was a sliding wooden door, behind which Father sat. On the other side of Father would be someone else, some other penitent, somebody one would pretend not to know, pretend not to be trying to hear: in any case, irrelevant. In the sacrament only the essential was allowed: priest, penitent, and of course, hovering above us in a greater darkness: God.

I was lucky that I was put in the line for the young Irish priest who was in our parish only for a year. He had curly black hair, a face that was always flushed, a heavy beard that never seemed well-shaved: full, girlish lips, also red, and dark green, sorrowful eyes. He was beautiful, and we all knew it, but it was not something we would have said about a priest.

I opened the wooden door to my side of the confessional and knelt on the hard wooden kneeler. I could smell my own sweat, and residually, the priest's sweat, different from mine, adult, male. My heart pounded with dread. He slid the screen open. "Bless me father for I have sinned, I committed a sin of impurity with myself." The words were out in the world: cobalt-colored rings that spun in the air above my head and clanked together as they joined and then transpierced the plastic screen. And then, after that, there was only silence, a silence I found so dreadful I could only imagine the terrible words from the priest that would, any moment, fill it up.

Now I can feel only compassion for him. What could he have felt it was right for him to say to a six-year-old girl who confessed "impurity"? His mortification must have been immense. But was it equal to mine? If I was waiting for some words of enlightenment, none came. Only my penance: three Hail Marys. And the injunction to go in peace.

And I did, and I was radiant, walking with my perfectly folded hands to the altar to say my penance. It was as if I had been dipped into a sea of sheerest silver, and walked out into the sunlight, my body brilliant as the sun. Or as if my veins had been shot through with silver light, so that there was nothing in my body that partook of darkness, not the smallest cell. The question must be asked: would that radiance have been possible without the prior sense of defilement? And was it worth it? This source of the ideal of the fire of making that burns off all dross, cuts out all irrelevance, all excess, all that is not crystalline, each tone not exactly true, each carelessness or slippage or smut or smudge, each encroachment on the shining surface of even a speck of matter that has not been shot through.

A dance teacher, trying to show me the proper position for a plié, explained its importance by saying, "You must go down to come up." We believe that about so much in life, but what would it be like to have grown up with no sense of the necessity for self-abasement? Is contrition possible without self-abasement? And is forgiveness possible without contrition? And without the experience of having been forgiven, how would one learn to forgive? And would the world be better without the possibility of radiant purity? Endless forgiveness? Does this require lines of shivering six-year-olds, believing that they are bad? Then transformed into radiant creatures, ready to take in God? Radiant and ready for what they have been told will be the greatest day of their lives.

The night before the great day, my mother and I lay everything out for the morning. My grandmother had made my dress. It was a source of perverse pride, a pride all the more honorable for its pinch of disappointment. I wished I had had a dress whose skirt was magicked with under crinolines, whose amplitude was added to by rows of machine-made lace. At the same time, I understood my mother's contempt for that kind of display: "It's all right for Italians," and the superiority of my grandmother's creation: sprigged organdy with a drop waist: austere, Northern, a hymn to the power, the superiority of restraint.

My mother had written a check, which I brought into school in a crisp white envelope, for my First Communion prayer book, the size of a deck of cards, hard and shiny as if it had been shellacked, the virgin on the cover a vision (also pointing to the superiority of restraint) in silver blue against a dove gray background. On the inside of the cover: a little miracle, cut into the stiff cardboard a recess; a rectangular grotto for a tiny white plastic cross. The check also paid for my First Communion veil, which was provided, somehow by the nuns, who ordered identical ones for each girl communicant, preventing a hideous competitiveness in what should have been an almost sacramental accessory—the veil that mimicked their own, the one that marked them as brides of Christ. A sign of the power of the parish in the larger commercial world: there was a store in our Long Island town that devoted its Maytime display to First Communion pocketbooks and gloves. We bought a pair of see-through white gloves with sprigging that rhymed nicely with the organdy of my dress. And a pocketbook, white patent leather, with handles neither too short nor too long for my hands and wrists, and a satisfying gold clasp that shut itself with a finality as unquestionable as the Creed.

I remember waking up that morning, and the quality of the light, opalescent, heatless, with the fragility of the incorporeal. I didn't want to speak to anyone, as if even words were too fleshly for that day, and might, somehow, mar the perfect purity I longed to perfectly achieve. A sip of water, then my mother's unfamiliar attentions to my dressing: I was the child of a working mother and had long ago learned to dress myself. I was afraid to walk up the driveway, afraid to absorb the slightest blemish on my white shoes. So my mother pulled the car out of the driveway, and stopped for my father and me. At my insistence, there was silence in the car, and then a silent escort by my parents to our classroom, from which we would process, in a double line, across the street into the church.

Procession. Processing. The verb pronounced with an accent on the second syllable, indicating movement rather than the first, process indicating a patient, slow accomplishment. What is the pleasure of walking in a line, to music, behind others dressed identically to oneself, so obviously of the same cohort or tribe? Do I have to believe it is a species of militarism, the appeal of the proto-fascist in us all?

There is a home movie of me processing into the church. My father jumps out of the sea of onlookers when I pass him. Piously, I lower my eyes and shake my finger at him: there will be no vulgar familial communication on this day. In later life, my appetite for obedience will always be mixed by an equally strong impulse to rebel. But on that day, I am completely obedient, and there is nothing I want to do that will mark me as different from my colleagues. Jesus is coming to all of us—there is enough of Him to go around. As we are all perfect, there is no need to excel. It is an economy of plenitude in which no one can be left out, therefore no one need stand out.

Did I understand, as I was processing with my classmates, that this was the best part of it all? That the minute I crossed the threshold into the church the experience, having properly said to have begun, could rightly be said to have begun being finished? That the moment that the event went from being exterior (outdoors, brilliant) to being interior (inside the church, dim lit, enclosed), it was already over? And what is the connection between that reality and the fact that, indoors, we were less a spectacle? For I know perfectly well that I was aware at all times that we were being carefully watched; both in my imagination of the event, and in my experience of its actuality, I was watching myself being watched: I had a triple identity, I was the child, walking, kneeling, opening her mouth, I was myself watching that child among other identical children, and I was a member of the observing crowd, moved nearly to tears by the unique, the incomparable sight.

But when the church doors closed and the spring sunshine was occluded, and we were in the light reflected off the gray-green walls and the barn like beams of the Gothically vaulted ceiling, another kind of door was shut. I had to fix my entire attention on God: the God in the Host on the altar, the God whom I would take into my body, purified by hunger, by contrition, by the sacramental touch. "O Lord I am not worthy," that prayer, said just before we would receive, *Domine non sum dignus* in the Latin of the day, drew me like a magnet; my unworthiness, the incomparable unearned riches of the love of God.

There was still the possibility of failure. I was away from food; but I could faint. There were stories of children, always girls, who did, and had to be carried out and missed receiving. I both envied them the glamour of their ride in some man's arms, and was terrified that another kind of physical weakness—not from my stomach, but from my blood or brain or whatever controlled uprightness, consciousness—would disallow me from the great moment, the moment for which I had prepared for so long. Or I could trip on the way up to the altar, mortifying myself and my parents. Or I could choke on the host, or my teeth could touch it—this, I knew, was considered a sacrilege and in the very process of sanctification I could be involved in sin.

But then the moment came. I did not trip or choke; my hands were folded perfectly and the host slipped, like a silver fish into dark water, onto my tongue and down my throat.

After that, the world was banished from my sight, my mind. I lowered my eyes, concentrating them on the floor or the tips of my pointed, folded fingers. It was an agony to keep my eyes open while I was finding my place in the long pew. I longed only for darkness. For the moment I rehearsed: the screen I made of my two hands, the deeper darkness when I shut the blind of my two eyelids. I was alone with God. I said the prayer that I had memorized. I felt the love, the pity, the piercing, the numbering. I thanked God for coming into my soul, and I thanked God for my parents for making me a Catholic—and then I couldn't think of very much else. I might have thanked God for being an American or for my school and my extended family, but God knew and I knew that it was pro forma. The important things were that I had made my First Communion and that I was my parents' child—God and I knew my gratitude for those was real.

I had taken God in. My task was to experience the experience of having God within me. But trying to fix my mind on God, who was outside, beyond time, did not help my sick dread, the consciousness that it was being used up, this precious substance I had invested in for so long. Every moment was turning each succeeding moment into the Last of My First Communion.

After the memory of my first prayers behind the double screen of hands and eyelids, there is no memory: memory stops. There is a nullity, a blank. Did we process out "in an orderly fashion," or did we become ordinary children again, running to our parents willy-nilly, like any one at all? Was there some sort of celebration afterwards? I don't remember one, although I know that it was customary to have a party after First Communions. But there are no pictures of a party, only me, my parents, and my grandmother sitting on folding chairs in our driveway. My mother was incapable of organizing parties; did my grandmother feel she'd done enough making the dress, and my aunt, who didn't like me, but who made beautiful cakes—was she acting out her anger at me for existing on this special day? It doesn't matter. What could cake, sweet drinks, presents mean after what I had experienced? After what I had become?

Fifty years before the day of my First Communion, May 19, 1956, it would have been May 19, 1906. The First World War had not happened. Queen Victoria had just died. Henry James was still alive. The automobile had not been invented. *The Interpretation of Dreams* was six years old, as I was on the day of my First Communion.

It seems impossible that an identical number—50—denotes an identical number of years—50. Incomprehensible that the separation between 1906 and 1956 and 1956 and 2006 are the same. It is a strange thing that past-ness does not spread itself out, like cement on a slab to be smoothed over with a trowel creating a perfectly flat surface. If we think of someone now dressing in the style of Marilyn Monroe, if we should see a woman on the streets of New York in 2006 dressed in the halter dress from *The Seven-Year Itch*, we would think it amusing, stylish, but not so anachronistic as to be absurd. But in 1956 if a woman were wearing long skirts, high button shoes, huge picture hats—we would have thought her mad or known her costumed as someone who could not possibly be anything like herself. When I try to think of a movie star who would have been current in 1906, I remember that the concept of movie stars had not yet been invented. Impossible to imagine a world without the idea of a movie star. Without the moving picture, the image making its way through darkness to our porous brains. Was it the movies that divided time into the far past—everything we could not see filmed—and the accessible past, the past we can recapture? The long dream in the waiting dark, which can be seen and grasped again each time we choose to enter.

How will we know ourselves in fifty years? To whom and how will we be connected?

I know that, whoever I am, something lodged in me, or was lodged on that day. The taste for the invisible. What is felt in the body through charge and temperature, but unseen. A way that I can know myself. My highest self, the truest one, the one that ordinary life must, by its nature, blur and muddy.

It is the fiftieth anniversary of my First Communion. What was I then that I am still?

I am no longer a child. I am aware of all the things that are beyond me. Sister Trinitas' pitch pipe, playing the one right note, is rusted now, or lost, or buried with her—I do not even know if she is still alive. As an adult, I saw her once. Her hair was blonde; she was wearing a black and white hound's-tooth suit. I would not have recognized her. But always, the tone she started appears, then vanishes, then reappears. And I can see her face, white, beautiful pursing its lips, blowing on the instrument to make the tone.

Her lips on the pitch pipe started it: the longing for the tone. Its elusiveness. To find it is to return to the body of the kneeling child, behind the reddish screen, made by light penetrating the thickness, the flesh and blood blocking, but not entirely, the world.

She is alone and not alone, that child. She is and is not one thing only. She is a kneeling child, alive in a moment of time. But she believes she has taken into her body timelessness.

What will become of it, this timelessness? What will become of her?

Fifty years. More than half a lifetime. Half a century.

The knowledge that in fifty years she (I) will no longer be a body in the world.

Mary Gordon is the author of many books of fiction and nonfiction, among them the excellent Reading Jesus: A Writer's Encounter with the Gospels.

I HEAR AND BEHOLD GOD IN EVERY OBJECT, YET UNDERSTAND GOD NOT IN THE LEAST

Pattiann Rogers

For God so loved the order of things that he gave his only begotten son that whosoever believes in him should not perish . . .

So Jesus said, according to John.

God so loved the world, loved the order of things, loved the earth, loved the order of the earth, loved us as creatures born of the order of things, born of the stars and the order of the stars, born of the earth born of the stars, made of the stars, made of the earth.

I fall into the beauty of that song and momentarily I am saved. I do not perish.

I agree with Walt Whitman: *I hear and behold God in every object, yet understand God not in the least.*

Maybe the creative order of the universe—those massive stars, the super novae, those super stars smelting in their nuclear furnaces all the elements from which every body in the universe is composed, the planets gathering those elements to become themselves, the earth slowly forming, core and mantle, mountains rising, tectonic plates shifting, the great oceans of the earth churning for billions of years until the first flickering grip of life begins, those first, daring, determined, primordial creatures coming and coming—maybe the processes of this order resulted ultimately in the birth of a certain child who came to be called the Christ. Perhaps the universe brought forth in love this child who uttered those words. Maybe this was the way it happened— the order of things, the universe, the love embodied in creation bringing forth this fruit.

I don't know how it happened. But here it is, our earth and the heavens, those words, the story of that life, that resounding message. And isn't it true that love enhances, gives health and energy, causes the capacity for good to expand, is kin to joy, a cousin to reverence, while hate hinders, withers its host, promotes destruction, brings anger and misery, nurtures the well-being of nothing?

Love is a creative force in the physical world. We are agents of love and its witnesses.

Jesus Christ could not have lived without love, the Christ story could never have been conceived by anyone without love, the words themselves would never have existed without love, and without the words and a speaker of words this story could not have been told. *God is love*, He is said to have said. Maybe love was what was there before the beginning, before the Big Bang. Maybe love is the creative power within the order of things. Maybe love is the way of the universe. I could take the beauty of that into my heart.

Consider the lilies of the field, how they grow: they neither toil nor spin, and yet I say to you that even Solomon in all his glory was not arrayed like one of these. Those words of beauty were placed in their order by a poet in love with the earth. *Not one sparrow falls to the ground that God is not aware.* Those words of honor were composed by a poet in love with the life of the earth. *The meek shall inherit the earth.* Who better to receive with love the order of the earth?

Maybe a child born of love who then loves wholly, purely, perfectly, with all his heart and all his soul and all his mind, can walk on water, can give sight to the blind, can rise again from the dead, can be this attuned with the creative love within the order of things. That child, the gift of the universe, would be love in human form. Maybe this is how love conceived itself.

I am in love with the life of the earth, the hundred budding eyes seeking light in a water-buried nest of tadpoles, a tomato on the vine basking from blossom to ripe red, in love with our enormous, frightening sun and all creatures basking in the light of its being, a green anole invisible on a green leaf, a yellow-striped garter snake curled on a smooth stone, in love with the fragrance of a river when a summer evening begins to cool and the cicadas and crickets strike up their buzz and jingle in the poplars and shore grasses. I'm in love with the cosmic heaven, its terrible, haunting glory, its racing explosions and dangerous maelstroms of burning rocks and dusts and great arcs of glowing gases, in love with the silence of that same sky above midnight snow, the white land and its barren shadows drenched in the pale blue stillness of the moon; in love with the order of things, crystals adhering piece by icy piece, a single, widening furl of campfire smoke, electrons and atoms, ocean currents and the rhythmic currents of blood through the bodies of living creatures and the rhythmic currents and waves of a veering flock of ricebirds over the fields, the sweep of porpoises veering through the swell of ocean waves; and our own creations, the written language of musical scores, bells and drums, wax whistles and pianos, hot air balloons, bicycles, roller blades, calculus, arboretums, *Voyager* I and *Voyager* II, and all voyagers traveling to the constant night of the ocean floors or to the airless glacier peaks of mountains or into the realms of the nano world, actors, artists, acrobats, archivists, a quilt spread on the grass, supper on a quilt spread on the grass, in love with our words alone in an otherwise wordless universe (as far as we know), in love with *as far as we know*, in love with *amen*.

All of us want to be loved unconditionally. We crave that love. We are born craving to be loved unconditionally. Some of us become warped and crippled from the lack of that love, some of us become stunted, some of us sicken, some of us die from the lack of that love. Maybe the health and vibrancy of the universe too depend on a love like that. Maybe the creation is not finished. Maybe the creation, in its ongoing shifting and changing, altering and evolving, requires a robust strength that love alone can provide, a love given freely and unconditionally throughout the coming and going of stars and mountains and suns and planets, in the coming and going of life. We know we are a source of love. We know we have the ability to receive and to give love, to sustain by giving love. We can love the order of the world, receive and acknowledge with love its gifts of life and beauty and one another. We can express love to a universe that requires it, give love despite fear, despite horror and grief, despite suffering, despite our ignorance, love unconditionally despite death. Each of us can give that gift as we are able. I want this gift to be received. I want to participate in the creation in this way now, wherever *now* might be, in place, in time, among the countless and the far beyond.

Pattiann Rogers has written in Portland Magazine *of rain, grace, water, grief, and stars. She is the author of many books, among them* Song of the World Becoming, *her collected poems.*

The River

Paul Myers

Many years ago I was fishing in the Wilson River with my brother-in-law. It was autumn, salmon season. The air and the river were cold and you could smell the sea. Yellow and gold and bronze leaves darted and swirled and spun in the crystalline waters at our feet. Morning mist hung in the hemlocks and firs climbing the mountains. Everywhere there was mottled light.

I heard the sound of plastic hitting rock and I looked over and saw my brother-in-law lean over to retrieve his lure box from the river and then he slipped and fell in and the river yanked him away. He groped frantically for the rocks and jabbed his heels desperately into the river-bed and after a second or two he actually stood up, the pounding water fanning out behind him high and wide as a peacock's tail; and then the river grabbed him and pulled him straight down into its bosom and he vanished.

I dropped my gear and ran as fast as my waders would allow, ducking and shoving through alder and vine maple and devil's club, and I clambered up on the boulder where he had been seconds ago but there was nothing in the river but his hat.

I screamed his name again and again and again and again and again. His hat whipped away down the river.

Please God help please God

I read that water desperately, anything, a ripple of him, any hint of his life, any hint of his body, his color, his face.

Please God please

I don't know how much time went by, a minute, two minutes, and then I noticed a thick tree branch jammed in the backwater at the head of the gorge. A sparrow lit on a ledge above the branch and then launched upriver just inches over the riffles. The branch rolled a bit and I realized it was his leg, and I screamed his name, I screamed and screamed, but his head was underwater and he was dead.

Please God help me

I ran downstream to the footbridge and ran across and climbed down to a dozen feet above him and yelled and pleaded. I went a little mad maybe. I wanted to throw rocks and sticks at him, pry him loose, throw some of my life at him and into him.

Please God

I ran up to the highway and waited forever with my heart pounding. There was a moment when I felt, with every fiber of my being, that his spirit, his soul, was rising out of the canyon. I cannot describe how sacred that moment was, how absolutely sure his soul was departing his body and rising up over the waters.

He was the happiest man alive, my brother-in-law. He had said so hours before. He and his wife were expecting their first child in two months. They had just purchased their first house. He had finally landed his dream job. His beloved college football team was going to the Rose Bowl. He was going to fish for salmon with new fishing gear that he had waited years to afford. He was beaming.

A water ouzel landed a few inches from his body and jumped back and forth into the river, catching breakfast.

Cars stopped. Finally there were eight men. Some had been fishing for salmon at the coast. Some had been crabbing in the bay. One was a New York City fireman on vacation.

We went to get the body. The fireman tied a rope around his own body. We lowered him down to the body. We dug our feet into the sand and gravel for leverage and hauled the fireman and my brother-in-law out of the river. By now search and rescue teams and emergency medical technicians and the deputy sheriff were there. They cut his boots off and tried to resuscitate him but he was dead.

We carried him up the steep uneven trail to the highway. An ambulance roared thirty minutes to the nearest hospital. I could not speak. A doctor pronounced him officially dead. I was led into a chapel. A minister came and sat with me and we prayed aloud. I wept and wept and wept until I was exhausted.

I cannot articulate how much pain I have felt and seen in the fourteen years since I saw my brother-in-law die in front of me. I loved that man, and I weep over the scars his sudden death caused his wife and child and clan. I cannot articulate the dark swirl of emotions and feelings and agonies in me since that moment. I cannot explain how hard I have tried to live up to the kind and generous and compassionate words people have said to me about his sudden death, my utter helplessness. I cannot explain how many thousands of hours I have asked God why my brother-in-law was taken so tragically, why I was chosen to witness such a horror.

I have never written about his death before, and I struggle to do so now; but after years of struggling and healing and praying, I tell you my story. I was witness to a moment of incredible holiness and I can no longer lock that up inside of my heart. I saw a man's soul leave his first temple and rise toward his next temple. I saw him depart from this planet.

I will see his face and hear his voice again, and that will be a joy I cannot understand. But I know that it will come.

Paul Myers is the author of many essays about students and miracles in Portland Magazine.

NATIVE

Notes on Americanness.

Ian Frazier

THE IDEA OF THE NATIVE PEOPLES of the Americas has been charged and complicated since the moment of first European contact with what the Europeans called, and we still call, the New World. The strength of the fantasy that we projected on this continent was such that it made the people here feel almost invisible, and made them very hard for us to see—and still does. In a real way you can say that modern American life and literature still depend very heavily upon that fantasy, upon encounters with the unknown, encounters with strangers, encounters exactly like those which characterized the birth of the United States many thousands of years after this land was populated by Americans.

Lately I've been reading Defoe's *Robinson Crusoe* with my children. You know the story, which is based on an account written by a real man named Alexander Selkirk who was stranded on an island off Argentina. At one point in the novel, Crusoe is walking on the beach and he sees a human footprint in the sand. This is an incredible moment for him. He's terrified, and his first reaction is to hide; he doesn't want to risk running into the strangers who have come to his island. It never occurs to him that he is the stranger and someone else, a native, is terrified of *him*. The novel is told completely from the point of view of the European, which is one of the reasons it was so popular in Europe when it first appeared. But that's not at all the way the real encounter took place in history; the real danger was Crusoe, the European, whose footprints would be followed by incredible death and destruction of the native people.

There were perhaps sixty million people living in North and South

America at the time of the first European contact. Four hundred years later, as the 20th century opened, censuses counted a quarter of a million living descendants of those sixty million. There had been a gigantic, terrifying, die-off of Native Americans. And at that time people thought that those 250,000 men and women and children were the last remnant, and soon they would be gone; Edward Curtis's famous pictures of the Last Native Americans were conscious efforts to record people who weren't going to be here anymore. He wanted to get photographs of them before they became extinct. He wasn't alone in expecting their extinction; I found an editorial in an 1877 issue of *The New York Times*, on the subject of Indian reservations, that actually said, in effect, that the Indians are going to die out, so let's at least let them die out on the land they love.

A cold and scary thought, and I am happy to report the die-off didn't happen. In the 1990 census there were more than two million Americans who identified themselves as Native Americans, which, in census-speak, makes them one of the fastest-growing ethnic groups in the country.

But there is no dispute that the arrival of Europeans on this continent was a disaster to the people who were here, and again I blame fantasy, even before smallpox, which killed most of them, and violence, which killed most of the rest. In some cases the fantasy was hopeful—here are people who are wholly free, the noble savage, depicted like Roman emperors, in their togas of furs and skins, striking the poses of classical statuary. In other cases the fantasy was that "Indians"—even the common name is a fantasy—were inhuman, un-Christian, deserving of no more consideration than you would give an animal. The Christian minister Cotton Mather, whose name is still written with respect in our history books, was of the opinion that the Native Americans should be wiped out as you would rid your garden of weeds.

The fantasy remains, for all we think we are sophisticated and sensitive these days. The mascots and logos of sports teams featuring the angry faces and dancing bodies of American Indians, for example—pretty derogatory and insulting. The Washington Redskins? Chief Wahoo, the mascot of my beloved boyhood Cleveland Indians? Yet those teams, and so many others, do not change their names, because the Native American demographic, at two million people, is simply too small to protest effectively. It's that simple.

In 1874 the Lakota chief Red Cloud gave a speech in New York City, at Cooper Union, and people there went crazy—they lined Fifth Avenue just to watch him walk by. His speech was reprinted in newspapers and made him a star. It made people fall all over themselves trying to help the Sioux. As a result of his enormously successful speech, the federal government made very generous concessions to the Sioux in a treaty that was signed shortly after that time. The treaty stated that the Lakota owned huge parts of the American Northwest, including the Black Hills of South Dakota, a holy place for the Sioux. And about twenty minutes after the treaty was signed, gold was discovered in the Black Hills and the treaty was promptly broken. The government found itself in a tough spot; it is very hard to stop a gold rush, hundreds of thousands of people rushed into the Black Hills, and for a while the government stationed soldiers around the hills to keep prospectors out, but that didn't last long. By 1875, not long after Red Cloud's speech, the hills were filled with white prospectors illegally taking gold worth millions of dollars from Sioux land. The government, to its small credit, tried to buy the hills back (not for a generous sum, either), but the Sioux declined.

Violence and argument ensued. The government decided that the solution was to require all Sioux and Cheyenne peoples to move onto reservations by January 1, 1876. The Sioux were already split among themselves about reservation life versus free life; those who came in to the reservation got food, heat, cash, and coffee (and one thing I learned about the Lakota then and now is that they do like coffee). Those who stayed out on the prairie sneered at the reservation Sioux as prisoners, sell-outs, chickens.

The government sent U.S. Army troops to bring the off-reservation people in. There were three military expeditions. One was led by the storied General George Custer, who found a huge group of Sioux (some 5,000 or so) at one encampment, a tremendous gathering for this nomadic people. Custer, perhaps dreaming of a huge victory that would propel him to the presidency he craved—remember that this is 1876, the nation's centennial, and a resounding military victory, then as now, is great political fodder—attacked with his 276 soldiers. The Sioux killed him and all the men with him.

Interstate highway 90 goes right past the Battle of the Little Bighorn site, and you can look up in the hills as you go by and see the grave markers where Custer's men were found. Evan Connell, in his great book *Son of the Morning Star,* describes how the rest of the Army realized what had happened to their colleagues. When Custer's detachment vanished, the Army sent a second unit to the battlefield. From a place fairly close to where the highway now runs, those soldiers looked up and saw a great deal of something white flashing on the ridge. For a moment some wondered if it was snow. But it was July and there was no snow. The scattered bits of white were the bodies of Custer's soldiers.

Custer was there with his brother, his brother-in-law, his nephew, a correspondent from *The New York Herald*, and a lot of people that he liked to hang out with. He loved newspaper coverage and he was great copy and he knew it well. He had lovely long blond hair which he was reluctant to cut, and whenever he did get a haircut his wife saved the locks that fell and made a wig of his hair for herself. She liked to wear the wig of his hair when they went to shows on Broadway. They'd have been on the cover of *People* magazine, George and Elizabeth Custer, if there'd been a *People* magazine then.

Custer only had one tactic—*charge!*—which he used throughout his career. During the Civil War, his wife, Elizabeth, met President Lincoln on a receiving line.

"Oh, your husband is the man who leads his troops into battle with a whoop and a hurrah," said Lincoln.

"And I hope he always will, Mr. President," said Elizabeth.

"Then you wish to be a widow," said Lincoln. And indeed Mrs. Custer was a widow far longer than she was a married woman. She died in 1932, having devoted her life to keeping the myth of her husband's greatness alive.

When the news of the Battle of Little Big Horn arrived at the Centennial Celebration in Philadelphia that summer, everyone was crushed. It had been an exciting and successful exhibition, something like a World's Fair. The telephone had been introduced to the public during the Celebration. People had spoken on the phone for the first time. You could speak to someone all the way across the crowded and bustling fairground. It was a miraculous thing. In many ways the Celebration was the beginning of the modern era in America. But news of the Little Big Horn cast an immediate and thorough pall on everyone.

The question of who owned the Black Hills was settled immediately. A year later the Black Hills had become federal property (purchased for almost nothing, the Sioux forced to sign by threat of having their rations withheld). Sioux reservations were greatly reduced in acreage, and the Hills were legally open to prospectors. This theft—for theft it was—

would resound through history. It still does; the case still has not yet been resolved, in large part because the Sioux to this day refuse to negotiate for anything less than the sacred land they wanted in the first place.

Very nearly every Sioux man, woman, and child on the plains was rounded up and forced onto reservations, and the subsequent years of famine and disease were brutal. By 1890 misery was so endemic that Indians all over the West were ripe for any kind of idea that would offer salvation. So up rose the Ghost Dance, a sort of religious revival and political rebellion at once. It started with a Paiute man in Nevada named Wovoka, who spoke to God, and he reported that God's message to the Indians was that they should continue their traditional ways of living, and begin a new, more devoted kind of dancing. Dancing and right living would bring back the buffalo and restore the Indians to their original strength. Dancing and right living would bury the whites with earth five times as deep as a man. The dance caught on quickly and flew from reservation to reservation. The Sioux, cautiously, sent a man named Kicking Bear to talk to Wovoka. Kicking Bear reported that he had looked in Wovoka's hat and seen the whole world, the whole vision, and that Wovoka spoke truly. So the Sioux began to dance.

I think it is safe to say that if any tribe would take something to the limit—dancing, for example—it would be the Sioux. They danced and danced and danced. There are photographs of the Sioux dancing in huge circles, dancing for days, falling down in trances and exhaustion, rising up and dancing some more. Some reported that they had danced so hard that they had flown to the morning star and brought back pieces of it. Some reported that they had seen and spoken with their dead relatives. Some dancers painted the visions they had seen, often on beautiful white shirts, and soon it was reported that a shirt with a vision painted on it was bulletproof. There are reports of people wearing the shirts and having guns fired at them point-blank and not being injured. I don't know how this could happen but that is what was said.

Talk of bulletproof shirts scared people. The Pine Ridge reservation Indian agent, a man nicknamed Young Man Afraid of the Sioux, called for Army reinforcement. The Army sent the Seventh Calvary—Custer's unit. This is fourteen years after Little Big Horn, but memories on both sides were fresh. Disaster followed. A Sioux leader named Big Foot and his people, reportedly heavily armed, are camped at Wounded Knee

Creek. The Army goes in to disarm them. There is a struggle and shots are fired. The soldiers, up on a rise around the canyon of Wounded Knee Creek, fire down at the Indians with exploding shells. The Indians are massacred. Hundreds of Indians and dozens of soldiers are killed, some of the soldiers by friendly fire.

When I was working on a book about the Sioux, I went to the Plains and read as many newspapers of the time as I could find. There were lots of newspapers in the West then. I believe there were more newspapers per capita than there are now. I found one newspaper in South Dakota where L. Frank Baum, later famous as the author of *The Wizard of Oz*, complained that the massacre at Wounded Knee wasn't enough, and that a sensible government would just wipe all the Indians out and be done with it. I found another article by a then-famous humorist named Bill Nye, who wrote a humor piece about the massacre. There was more like that. I was staggered.

This is the tradition of American journalism that modern journalism, and to a degree modern politics, is still reacting to. The tendrils of history are much longer than we admit. From the widespread attitude at first contact, that Indians were animals without souls, to the attitude not all that long ago that they should just be exterminated . . . it was because of clearly expressed intentions like these that Native American activists of the 1960s and 1970s used the word *genocide*, loud and long, and it is hard to argue with their use of that word. We see that word a lot these days, often to describe events in such battered African nations as Rwanda and Sudan, but we do not see it used as much for such a battered people as Native Americans.

Sometimes that which is closest to us we don't see at all. I feel a certain responsibility as an American writer to try to see that which is closest to me in my country, which might explain why some of my books are about fishing and New York City or about Ohio and my family or about the Sioux, especially, a remarkable and paradoxical group of my countrymen. I have no patience with people, and there have been some, who say that I should not have written a book about the Sioux, because what could I, given who I am, really know? My answer there, I guess, is, well, as a middle-aged white guy, what *do* I write about? Other middle-aged white guys? Do we really want to know more about middle-aged white guys? We already have quite a few books and movies and plays and articles and political parties filled with middle-aged white guys. It is really essential for me to add to that? Isn't there something else that a chronicler of his or her time is asked to do?

It seems to me that to say you are only qualified to write about yourself is an easy excuse, and then the next step is to say you are only qualified to *read* about yourself, and pretty soon no one is learning anything about anyone, and so we all learn nothing about suffering and grace and courage, and that would be a seriously bad idea.

When I traveled around the Sioux reservation doing my research for my book, I saw Elvis Presley posters everywhere. I remember spending a day with one man who told me, as we drove around, about one disaster after another on the reservation: *Here's where there was a terrible car wreck, here's where a guy got his head blown off, here's where a bomb went off*, etc. It was horrifying. Then he says, "But I'll tell you the *really* hard time here on the reservation, the saddest time of all—August 1977."

I ask, my God, what happened in August 1977?

"What *happened*?" he says in disbelief. "Elvis died!"

I heard a story on the reservation that I will remember all my life. It's about a girl named Sue Anne Big Crow. She played for the Pine Ridge girls' high school basketball team. They played a game against Lead, a nearby town, where there was more than a little racism against the Lakota. Lead was a gold mining town—mining land, you will remember, stolen from the Lakota. As the Pine Ridge girls run onto the court, they're heckled and yelled at by the Lead fans. Sue Anne leads the Pine Ridge girls onto the court. But she stops at center court, facing the Lead fans, drapes her warmup jacket over her shoulders, and does the Lakota shawl dance. She started to sing, too, in Lakota. And something happened; the crowd went silent, and all you could hear was Sue Anne singing, and everything changed. Her friends said afterwards that what she did was make Lakota relatives of everyone in the gym that day. She died a couple years later, in a car wreck, and there's a recreational center in Pine Ridge named for her. She didn't drink, she didn't do drugs, she was very opposed to both in a situation where it was difficult to be opposed to them. That was Sue Anne.

Another thing I have learned, in talking to Sioux and other Native American people all over this country and up into Canada, is that all Native American people have pretty much the same accent. I can't explain it. I pick up the phone and on the other end can be a friend from Alaska or Canada or South Dakota or Florida and the accent is the same. Makes you wonder, doesn't it?

We white people, we descendants of the Europeans who arrived here four centuries ago and since—we immigrants—have faced the same question all that time: Are we going to try to get rid of the people who were here before us, or try to make them stronger? We haven't decided which to do. Sometimes it seems to me that the reservations are essentially prisons, and the people there are essentially trapped. And I know that all too often the reservations are places of terrible alcoholism, and that if we—our government and the companies like Anheuser-Busch that trumpet their community service—took our own words seriously, we might open a few alcohol treatment centers on the reservations—for example, on the Pine Ridge reservation, which has none, zero, zilch. Yet the populations on reservations are growing, despite the difficulties of living there, while populations in white towns on the Plains are dying out. The implication is interesting. Perhaps the middle of the United States will someday be like Utah, where Mormon culture and Mormon religion dominate. Perhaps someday the Plains will be a great Lakota Nation, with great schools, famous universities, terrific athletes, great artisans and writers and civic leaders. Perhaps someday there will be a great number of people who call themselves Lakota-American. Perhaps someday the terms Native American and American Indian will die out, and history texts will explain that it took five hundred years for tribal people and later arrivals to figure out how to live together in this extraordinary land between the oceans.

Ian Frazier is the author of many books, among them the classic Great Plains *and the remarkable* On the Rez, *about the Lakota people of middle America. This essay is drawn from his remarks to a University media and society class, hosted by journalism professor Mick Mulcrone.*

ACROSS THE VOID

A note on crazy and crucial hope.

ROBIN CODY

I DRIVE A BUS FILLED WITH JUVENILE DELINQUENTS to a reform school. These kids, "at risk" kids is the polite term, have been so disruptive in their neighborhood schools that the district assigned them to a dreary set of medium-security classrooms out on Marine Drive. This is their last chance to attend school while living at home. Their next stop might be the Mac—the MacLaren Youth Correctional Facility, in Woodburn.

I chose this route because the hours are good and boredom is not a problem. My passengers are teenagers, old enough to have stories of their own and occasionally unmoody enough to spill them. Sad stories. Or, no, the beginnings of good stories, maybe. Stories that I'd like to turn around and play backwards, so Dad comes home, Mom kicks her meth habit, and the cops turn out to be good guys after all.

You'd like to step in. Do something about this. Anybody would.

But I am fifty years older than they are. I don't like their music and I don't know an X-Station from a PlayBox. It's hard to understand their language and they don't get mine. It's not just the words but how an elder tries to use words to bridge a yawning socio-cultural chasm to reach a youngster he'd like to help. They don't dislike me. We are curiosities to one another, failing to connect.

"I don't need to read."

Yes you do. Everybody needs to read.

"I'm going to be a welder. My uncle's a welder and he makes $32 an hour."

Welders need to read the instructions. Work orders. The sports section.

"My uncle can't read."

Or you'd like to strangle them. Anybody would.

Take this knucklehead with swagger and shades who imagines himself the bull seal of the bus. I'll call him Dejarvis. He began rapping aloud one morning to vivid lyrics on his CD player about killing cops and screwing people. "Run, nigger, run. POW. POW."

Others, laughingly, picked it up in chorus.

They paid no mind to my reasoned pleas. Give me a break. This is inappropriate language. Weak stuff like that.

At school I secured the bus and went chest to chest with Dejarvis to block his exit. We exchanged ill-chosen words and then stood there surprised, eyeing each other unbudgingly—perhaps comprehendingly—across the void.

They wouldn't be on this bus if they didn't have a tortured relationship with school. And most of them have a fractured home life. They live with a grandparent or an aunt or a step-someone. Of the four boys and two girls on my route right now, only two have the same surname as an adult of the house.

A sullen pale teenager with zits and a bad haircut comes to the bus from a shabby house with its screen door off the hinges and a broken TV set in the neglected yard at an outer Southeast neighborhood known to bus drivers as Felony Flats. Reeking of cigarettes and resentment, he has been sentenced to this demeaning short bus that teenagers city-wide call a "retard bus." It kills him to be seen getting on or off it. Would you expect him to have a sunny disposition?

Or this. On a dry run to drop a time card for a new student, I come to a large, well-tended old house set back from Woodstock Boulevard behind two tall firs and a neat lawn. A foster home. Two cheerful teenagers rush to answer my knock. No, Teresa's not here. Yes, she lives here. They call for Tom, a bright young dad-like guy. Tom and I are on the veranda with paperwork. I expect to pick up Teresa at 7:58 each morning and bring her back by 3:40, starting Thursday.

But here comes Teresa now, from the sidewalk and up the front steps. She sizes me up—a stranger with picture ID—and I see pure terror in her lovely dark eyes. Teresa clings to Tom's elbow, pleading, and says to him, "Are they going to take me away?"

Imagine. It's not a Mom and Dad and the kids home, but Teresa has found a home here. She has an adult elbow to cling to, yet her world is so fragile.

. . . They're kids. They're unfinished human beings. You never know. It turns out Dejarvis can be civil and funny when he wants to be. He's a smart guy, older than the others, and on the bus we talk basketball. He plays ball. I doubt if he truly believes that his bus driver has played and coached and refereed hoops. But we unwrap some language we both understand. The school has a team, he tells me. Yes, there are twelve of these alternative schools in the metro area. League play will begin in January.

Well, shoot. I wonder. Maybe I'll shake out the old striped shirt and get on the court with these jokers.

"O.K., Robin," says a girl. "Last night? Guess what."

You apologized to your aunt?

"No."

What?

"Her stepson came over."

Is that good or bad?

"Good! We got a decent meal. We had steak on a stick. Squares of meat. We had that and corn and mashed potatoes!"

Come January and basketball practice, Dejarvis didn't come to the bus for five days in a row. Hoping he was just sick, I asked at school. What's up with Dejarvis? The principal told me Dejarvis got sliced up in that melee at Lloyd Center I'd read about in the paper. "He'll be back when he gets out of the hospital."

I didn't know Dejarvis was a gang member.

"You didn't?!" said the principal.

They come and they go. Why should I care? I drive them to school on a gray wooly morning, windshield wipers batting at a persistent mist. They wear their despair like two-G gravity blankets, and there's a vacancy in my chest where concern should be. Just get them to school. But we were early this morning. The staff won't open the school doors to this bunch until precisely 8:40, so I re-route onto Bridgeton Road, along the Columbia River dike.

Drop the headphones, people. We're taking the scenic route.

These garage-looking structures on the water are where rich people keep their yachts. Over there, that's Tomahawk Island. Those are some really important yachts. The ones with tall poles are sailboats. Hoist a sail up that pole when the wind is right and you can go on your boat without a motor. And these here are houseboats. People live here.

"Nice places."

I stopped the bus for a better look. This neighborhood is not exotic to me, but to them we were in Dubai, or Lake Oswego.

"What if the water come up?"

These houses float. The sidewalks, too. When the river rises, everything floats up. A few years ago, rivers got really high and a string of houseboats broke away. A whole neighborhood went floating down the Willamette River. I saw this on Channel 2. It was pretty exciting.

"What happened?"

They floated away. Nobody knows what happened. The river goes out to the ocean, you know? Houseboat people could be still floating around out there, eating their dogs, their cell phones out of range.

They were all quiet. I saw their wide eyes in my overhead mirror. Uh-oh. Broken kids can't tell when I'm putting them on. I once told Morris he'd better knock it off because he was sitting in the ejection seat. Poor kid, he believed me.

Now I pulled up to the school, but I didn't open the bus door.

No, wait. I remember. What happened was tugboats came to the rescue. They lashed those houseboats to the bank. When the water went down, they put the houses back up the river where they belonged.

"Aw, maaaan."

Aw, man, was right. By telling them what really happened, you see, I had ruined a believable-to-them story. These kids know in their bones that they have come unmoored from the world, and no help is on the way.

But you never know. Many of these kids are doomed by their circumstances, but you can't give up on them. Help is there, if they'll put in the work. Teachers and staff at this school are as gung-ho and brave as soldiers in Baqouba or Kabul, and more forbearing. Students get close attention and door-to-door transportation and breakfast. This is a year-round school. It's expensive, but the school will rescue some kids.

A tall disengaged beaten-down girl who avoided eye contact on my bus found a teacher who encouraged her ability to draw. She got the idea she should work at it. She did. And then, boy, could she *draw*. After months of smart work and good behavior, she earned her way back to Madison High. On her last day with us she passed out Snickers bars to everyone on the bus.

Or this. A foul-mouthed and sharp-tempered boy swallowed, hook, line, and sinker, the school's three-step program from Safety to Respect to Responsibility. He, too, got the idea it was up to him. He loosened up and began to get along. He even felt free to needle me—me—about appropriate language and anger management.

"Robin, I know a good case worker for you."

You win some and you lose some. I lost Dejarvis. Basketball season had begun by the time he came back from the hospital. Dejarvis joined the team and showed some skills, but he was out of shape. He played puffingly for a couple of games, lost interest, and quit coming to school.

Dejarvis is gone, but I referee basketball anyway.

At a dimly lit poorly ventilated crackerbox gym—here, come look—athletically gifted and under-loved street kids are hooping it up. And up. Some of them play above the rim. Some have stars in their eyes imagining NBA careers, and all of them run as if their shorts were on fire. Scores won't be reported in *The Oregonian*. There are no cheerleaders, but the girls cheer, yes they do. They rhythmically stomp and they musically chant and they groan in unison and they scream in delight.

It's hot in here. It's break-your-ankles fast in here. I whistle a foul and have to pause three or four beats for breath to say the call.

Now a guard makes a clean steal and breaks away. It's just him and the rim down court. The boy has springs, and he'll try to flush this one. He'll put some mustard on it and have maybe a 60 percent chance of scoring. Dribble one, dribble two, he's at the basket, and a gasp from the crowd sucks air from the court for this rim-rattling slam as he goes up with the ball . . . and with the tenderest most delicate touch lets the ball kiss off the backboard and fall gently to the net.

With sheep-eating grin, he turns back up court and glances winkingly at the coach who had been urging him all game to play under control.

You never know.

Basketball is a virtual world for some kids. Others escape to less healthy virtual worlds. On my bus I have come to know a parallel universe called *anime*, a Japanese computerized cartoon site reachable through hand-held gaming devices. *Anime* has blood and meanness, but it also fosters virtual alliances and tribal loyalty. A kid from a broken family can create a new family whole.

After school one day a burly buzz-cut boy who is given to tears anyway tromped onto my bus sobbing, choking. He slammed his backpack to the floor and head-butted the window while taking his seat.

What's the trouble, Jake?

"Devin said my wife is ugly."

In *anime*, you see, Jake has a wife and three children. This emotionally slippery boy administers virtual care and assigns chores. He is tough but fair. Others on my bus know that Jake's blustered desire to kill Devin for insulting his wife was an overreaction but not trivial. Jake is a family man.

Or this. A 15-year-old scatterbrained high-volume girl is always talking about her baby. She has no baby. But she tells me something new each day about her baby.

The baby has a birthday coming up.

The baby needs a checkup.

The baby died!

Sweet mother of Jesus. What would you do with this? I am not supposed to know, from the case worker, that the girl has had several "babies" who died.

After dropping her at home I have to park the bus and collect myself. It's bad form for a driver to return to the bus yard with tears in his eyes.

But there's basketball. Do come look. In this tiny grade-school gym, players go straight up for a lay-in to avoid collision with a wall at one end and a stage at the other. Suspended from the ceiling are square wooden backboards. We play twenty-minute halves with running time except for the last two minutes of each half. There are no bleachers. A single row of chairs fills up early, and then it's standing room only with deafening—but seldom rude—fans. Fans of rival gangs evidently have settled on a détente. Good humor and civil behavior rule. Ballplayers, too, are surprisingly compliant.

Maybe that's not so surprising. They don't have dads, remember. A man—even an old man—in a striped shirt gets their respect. I've taken more grief from over-indulged players and their parents at Lincoln High School than from these unloved boys of the street. It helps that my referee partner—the large easy-smiling Greg Taylor, who played college ball—knows what we're doing. And Portland police are at the door.

Wondrous athletic ability and wildly chaotic basketball are on display here. A popular offense is to fire up a three-point shot and crash the boards. But you know they've been coached because they play defense. They work on the high pick-and-roll, and I've seen a sweet bounce pass to a backdoor cutter that any high school coach in America would die for.

One slender point guard dominated a game while taking no more than three shots, just with slashing drives and deft passes. On a break he tossed the ball hard off the backboard for a trailing teammate to jam it. This boy has a withered right arm like a thalidomide baby. He gets fouled a lot and makes nine out of ten one-armed free throws. He understands the overarching beauty of basketball played well, and it just breaks your heart to see a kid so athletic and smart and to know he's in trouble.

That boy's team won the league championship. At the end of the game, we had a good ten minutes of unrestrained joy before coaches could corral the players for a trophy presentation. Kids did cartwheels and back flips. They hung off the rims. They bounced off the walls. Really. Two of these bad boys—too heavy for standing back flips—went running at the wall and up it to launch their 360s.

I am emotionally disturbed. I have witnessed the abandoned young of the species at the acme, the very pinnacle, of their lives so far. I want them to know more of this teamwork business, of getting along. But you throw a shipwrecked kid a life rope and there has to be something more to haul him in to. Family. School. Church. A job, maybe? I don't know. Basketball is not it, not in the long run.

On the morning after that final game's pure loopy joy, I learned about a robbery in the art room, where the winners had dressed. One of the boys claimed to have lost $300 and had kicked out a window at the school.

Wait. What?! This kid had three hundred dollars in his wallet?

The ups and the downs of caring for these people will turn you inside out, they are so extreme.

But here's upside news, that same morning: Dejarvis not only applied for but landed a job with Federal Express.

You never know.

Robin Cody, author of the novel Ricochet River *and the nonfiction classic* Voyage of a Summer Sun, *has written of rivers, salmon, courage, grace, and joy in* Portland Magazine.

MADRE DE DIOS
On the unimaginable ocean of Her love.

BARRY LOPEZ

I ENTERED A Jesuit prep school in New York City at the age of eleven and later finished two degrees at the University of Notre Dame. During those years in the city, I served regularly as an altar boy at Low Mass and also at Catholicism's most complex public ceremonies, including the solemn High Easter Mass, when the Paschal candle is ritually prepared and light begins to fill the cavernous dark of a cathedral, ending the purple-shrouded silence of Good Friday and Holy Saturday. At the Masses at which I served I felt no doubt or cynicism about what I was doing. Whatever my moods might have been, I believed and understood that I was in the presence of a great mystery.

As a freshman and sophomore at Notre Dame, I attended Mass three or four times a week. No matter what pangs of adolescence I might have been feeling then, and they were in my case severe, or whatever family troubles I might have been embroiled in, I felt the support and consolation of this Catholic ritual and the theology beneath it. Catholicism, though, was not a religion I was formally born to. I was baptized in the Church at the age of five, the son of a Roman Catholic father and a Southern Baptist mother. Soon afterward my father, a bigamist, abandoned my younger brother, me, and his spouse to return to his other wife and son. My mother—inexplicably, it would seem later—insisted on raising my brother and me as Catholics, though she herself would never convert. She supported us as a teacher and, years later, told me that the Catholic schools in California's San Fernando Valley back then were better than the public schools. Maybe for her that was all there was to it.

In college, I came to see that the Jesuits had encouraged in me a more metaphorical than literal understanding of Catholic liturgy, and that they had also encouraged me to develop an informed, skeptical attitude toward organized religion in general. The Jesuit approach to spiritual life, famously, was cerebral, but, importantly for me, theirs was a tradition also at ease with mysticism as a path to God. By the time I was thirteen—my mother had gotten remarried by then, to a twice-divorced Roman Catholic who moved us from California to New York—I had found a spiritual home in Catholicism. I reveled in Catholic iconography and ritual. I was fascinated by the difference between the regal Jesus of religious institutions and the historical Jesus. And I was a diligent student of the overarching Catholic history of medieval Europe (though not very well informed about the foul underbelly of the Crusades or the behavior of the Borgia popes).

At the end of my senior year in high school, I accompanied my classmates to a Jesuit retreat house at Cornell-on-Hudson, New York. I was fixated at the time on leading a life like Teilhard de Chardin's, the Jesuit paleoanthropologist, a life of inquiry into secular and sacred mystery, and a life of service to God and man. We spent three days in prayer, silence, and contemplation (as the Jesuits characterized it), in order to become more certain each of us was taking the right next step as we prepared for college. I hoped to return to the city convinced that my future lay with the Jesuits, but that was not what happened. I felt no calling. I entered, instead, the University of Notre Dame, declaring aeronautical engineering as my major.

It turned out that aeronautical engineering was not my calling either. By the middle of my freshman year, with some pointed advice from my physics professor, I came to see that I was enthralled not with the mechanics of engineering but with the metaphors of flight, with Icarus's daring and the aerial acrobatics of tumbler pigeons, which I had raised in California after my father left. I moved over to the College of Arts and Letters, and there took up writing, photography, and theater. At the time—the mid-sixties—every Arts and Letters undergraduate was required to take four years of philosophy and four years of theology. As the reading and classroom discussion in these particular courses went successively deeper, my understanding of the lives of mystics like Teresa of Ávila and John of the Cross expanded, along with my curiosity about what ordinary daily life was like for people like Francis of Assisi and Martín de Porres.

During my graduate and undergraduate years at Notre Dame, if I prayed in public at all, it was usually at a grotto on campus, a wide, shallow cavern of fieldstone built into a slope between the campus's two lakes. A statue of the Mother of God stood there on a pedestal above a barrier of wrought-iron pickets. It was flanked and fronted by dark wrought-iron stands on which racks of votive candles burned in deep-red and dark-blue glass vessels. The Grotto, as it was called, was lit day and night by these hundreds of flames. The flickering yellow light, swept regularly but rarely extinguished by gusts of wind, and so arranged as to not often be extinguished by rain or snow, represented for me the elusiveness of what had attracted me and others to organized religion, to that sphere of incomprehensible holiness which, in the Western imagination, stands beyond the reach of the rational mind. On some frigid nights when I knelt there, alone in the effervescent swelling of candlelight holding the darkness at bay, I felt a streaming convergence of inert stone, gleaming light, weather, and shadowed trees, all of it presided over by an unperturbed and benevolent Queen of Intercession, a woman hearing my prayers.

I drifted away from Catholicism my junior and senior years, though without anger or denouncement. Most of the friends I made at Notre Dame broke with the Church during their time there, but I did not experience the fury they felt, the sense of betrayal they described. (We were a decided minority at the school, listening to Bob Dylan in our dorms and protesting against the Vietnam War in our Carnaby Street bellbottoms.) My friends imagined themselves trapped in a risible and suffocating superstructure of religious doctrine, cut off from the very empirical experiences that could make for a full life. The Church, in their view, was asking them to embark on lives that had already been led.

I drifted away because the religion I sought was, finally, not to be found at Notre Dame. The environment in which we learned was not just exclusively male; hardly a single Protestant attended class with me, let alone an agnostic or Jew. No philosophy but that which had produced the culture of the West was examined. We were middle-class white youths, being taught to perpetuate our religious and economic values throughout the world. We were largely innocent of the world, however, so innocent it should have scared us.

When I graduated, I took a job with a publishing house in New York, but the question of both my vocation and my religion remained unsettled. A few months into my employment I asked for a week off and traveled to Kentucky, to make a retreat at Gethsemani, the Trappist monastery near New Hope where Thomas Merton lived. I wanted to address one more time the possibility of a religious life. This monastery, with its daily routine of liturgy and manual labor—it was a working farm—seemed a right place for me, a Cistercian community in the tradition of the French Carthusians and Benedictines. As attractive as I found the lives monks led there, however, the answer still seemed to be no.

In the decades following that decision to look elsewhere, I was fortunate to be able to travel often and widely, from Greenland to Tierra del Fuego, from Tajikistan to Namibia, from Poland to Tahiti. Much of what I would see, to employ a noun popular in some Catholic circles when I was young, was the culture of heathens, though these foreign epistemologies and metaphysics always appeared to me to be recondite and profound on reflection. In traveling with Alaskan Eskimos, with Kamba tribesmen in Kenya, and with Warlpiri people in the Northern Territory of Australia, I found a spirituality and a capacity to engage with mysticism that I have come to think of as a universal among people. The utility and strength of these ways, of course, is often obscured by the ordinary failure of every human society to live up to its own expectations. How a particular society reconciles its history of seemingly intractable failures, its strains of injustice and irreverence, with its spiritual longing for perfection is, to me, a succinct expression of its religion.

In those many years of travel, long after I had lost touch with my Catholic practice, I continued to rely, anyway, on the centrality of a life of prayer, which I broadly took to be a continuous, respectful attendance to the presence of the Divine. Prayer was one's daily effort to be incorporated within that essence. I continued to believe, too, in the immanence of the Blessed Mother, for me a figure of compassion and charity, a female bodhisattva (not meaning here to slight either strict Catholics or Buddhists). She was simultaneously a figure rooted in my religious tradition (including the tradition of the Black Madonna, of which the Church of my youth never spoke) and a figure who transcended religion. Like her Son, the battered Jesu nailed to a gibbet at Golgotha, she did not need a religion to inspire belief in her existence. Further, if one had any imagination, she did not need the papal bulls of Pius IX and Pius XII to gain credibility in the eyes of either a devout Catholic or apostate.

I have felt the presence of the Blessed Mother only twice.

I was in the northern part of the Galápagos Archipelago once, in

1989, passing just north of Isla San Salvador late on a May afternoon, when I saw a slight disturbance on the shoreward water, about a mile away. Just inside Buccaneer Cove, the low rays of the setting sun were catching what seemed to be the vertical strikes of blue-footed boobies diving for fish. The repeated splashes, however, were occurring only at one spot. With a pair of ten-power binoculars I finally made out a herd of sea lions trapped in a net.

We were on a course for distant Isla Genovesa, and I knew the captain might not want to detour. I located our guide, Orlando Falco. I gave him the glasses and he quickly confirmed what I thought—sea lions drowning in a net set illegally by local fishermen who intended to use the carcasses as bait to catch sharks. The sharks would have their fins cut away and then be turned loose to drown. (Over the past few days, we had seen four or five definned sharks washed up on Galápagean beaches.) The fishermen were selling the shark fins—another illegal act—to buyers aboard Asian factory ships who, as it happened, were supplying them surreptitiously with expensive nets and other fishing gear.

Orlando was conflicted. He said the captain, who was his employer, would be very reluctant to get involved in what would appear to be a judgment about the livelihood of other men on the islands, illegal or not; and he would not want to get caught up in Galápagos National Park politics. Nevertheless, we went to the bridge and he argued our case. The captain glared briefly at Orlando, then changed course.

Once the *Beagle III* was anchored in the cove, Orlando and a crewman lowered a motor-powered, fourteen-foot panga into the water and, with four other tourists traveling aboard the *Beagle*, we approached the sea lions. Some of them were trussed so tightly in the net's green twine that their eyeballs bulged from their heads. To get a short breath, one animal, closely bound to three or four others in a knot, might have to force the others underwater, only then to be driven underwater itself by another animal struggling to breathe. The high-pitched whistles and explosive bellows of animals gasping for air rent the atmosphere in the cove again and again. Their desperation and sheer size made an approach in the small panga dangerous, but we had no choice now. Orlando and I braced ourselves to work on the port side. Two people leaned out on the starboard side to balance the boat. The crewman kept the lunging jaws of the sea lions away from us with an oar blade, and Orlando and I went after the net with our knives.

I ran a hand under the constricting mesh, pulled it toward me, and began cutting. In their efforts to climb into the panga—they were biting frantically at the port gunwale to gain purchase—the animals threatened to pitch both of us overboard. How they had survived until now, I couldn't begin to understand. Braced hip-to-hip, Orlando and I cut away the twine, trying not to nick the sea lions' flesh. It was full dark by now on the equator, where dusk is brief. A second panga arrived with flashlights from the *Beagle* and stood away after handing them over. The light beams swept wildly through the night, catching the mesh pattern of the net, pink mouths, white canines, and the glistening conjunctivas of the sea lions' eyes. Orlando and I nicked our forearms and hands, and our shins cracked repeatedly against the boat's gunwale.

In the heaving chaos something yanked at the hilt of my knife—a sea lion flipper, the net—and it was instantly gone. Snatched into the night. Without it I could not continue to help. I was briefly paralyzed, then swung around to help Orlando. Someone was bailing the panga around my feet. Like a tightrope walker I reached out to maintain my balance. When I closed my empty hand in the dark air above the water, it closed around the haft of the knife. Orlando, adjusting his stance to accommodate me, saw the knife appear in my hand. He looked at me without expression and then fell back to work. Orlando and I became aware then that whenever our hands touched an animal, the moment it felt a knife sliding between the twine and its skin, it went limp, while the sea lions next to it continued to bawl and thrash. With this help from them we were able to work more quickly.

In the weak beams of the flashlights we could not be certain, but it seemed we finally freed about fifteen animals, all but one of which swam slowly away. Before we left, Orlando and I pulled ourselves hand-over-hand along the entire length of the float line all the way to the anchor buoy, cutting the net's mesh to shreds.

Back aboard the *Beagle*, everyone save Orlando and me stepped into the main cabin for a late dinner. The two of us sat on the open deck in silence, barefoot, our T-shirts and shorts soaked. Orlando, a young Argentine, was not a man particularly reverent about anything, certainly not mystical. In the deck lights we could see that our shins were turning black-and-blue, that the small cuts on our hands and arms were swelling shut from the salt water.

I said, "Did you see what happened with the knife?"

"La Madre de Dios," he said, staring into the night.

Later that evening, unrolling my sleeping pad on the *Beagle*'s deck, I recalled a single one of her many appellations; Mediatrix of Graces.

The other time I felt the Blessed Mother near, it was not another man's observation which I accepted without hesitation, a moment when something made perfect sense. It was thirty-six years earlier. I was eight years old, trapped in a pedophile's bedroom. This man, who first sodomized me when I was six, went on doing this until I was eleven. He enjoyed the complete confidence of other adults in our community. He commanded their respect as a medical doctor. I was a rag doll in his bed, an object he jerked around to suit himself. He had carefully arranged the many fears of my childhood life—insecurity, lack of physical strength, a desire to do the right thing—to create a cage. I could not see any way out.

That afternoon, gazing into the shabby bedroom in catatonic submission, I saw the Blessed Mother, a presence resolved in the stagnant air. She was floating barefoot a few inches above the floor, clothed in a white robe. Over her head she wore a pale blue veil. Her hands were extended toward me. She said, "You will not die here." I took her to mean that something else lay beyond this. As bad as it could still get, she seemed to be saying, she would be there.

The Queen of Heaven, I might have thought then. And would say now.

Among the many books of Barry Lopez are the masterpieces Winter Count, The Rediscovery of North America, *and* Arctic Dreams.

Who Am I, Lord, That You Should Know My Name?

A note on believing, against all sense and reason

BRUCE LAWRIE

MY SIX-YEAR-OLD SON and I share a nightly ritual, just the two of us alone in the fading light of his bedroom. Matty, who is severely mentally retarded, loves routine because life comes at him as if blasted from a water cannon, the millions of sights and sounds we all unconsciously assimilate every second of every day an undecipherable roar. Even more than most children, Matthew craves the safety that comes from learning the rhythms of his life, thrives on repetition. And of all his daily routines, winding down to bedtime might be the best. For a few minutes every night, I can turn down the white noise for him and help him ease into the peaceful joy of drifting off to sleep. We start out sitting on the floor with his favorite board book about monkeys drumming on drums, dumditty, dumditty, dum, dum, dum. . . . The book is worn with love, all four corners gnawed off—Matthew chews up books the way other kids do grilled-cheese sandwiches, starting at the corners and working his way to the center. As we reach the last dumditty on the last page, he lets out a sigh that tells me everything's right in his world and he's looking forward to climbing into bed.

I rise to my feet and begin singing, *Lord, I lift your name on high* . . . as I reach down to help him into bed.

He's unable to walk on his own but he can aim himself in the general direction of the bed. He knows where this is heading and he's ready for it. He pauses at the bedside to feel the blankets and pillow for a moment as if to make sure the bed is still stationary. Legally blind in one eye, he's learned that things have a disturbing way of disappearing right when you're ready to lean on them. But, as always, he finds the cool sheets safe, slings a skinny leg over the bed, and hauls himself up on top, moving rapidly before the bed can escape. He lies on his back rocking back and forth in bed, body rigid, a crease-eyed smile lighting his face, letting out an ecstatic aaahh.

I turn out the light and kneel beside his bed in the dark room, still singing, *You came from heaven to earth.* . . .

Matty holds his arm out in my -direction, a tentative groping for me in the sudden blackness. I wrap his hand in mine and press it to my face. I start singing the next song in our nightly rotation as I brush his hand against my whiskers, first his palm and then the back of his hand. He explores my face with his fingertips and then he covers my mouth gently. I sing into his palm, imagining the reverberations vibrating down into his little soul. How does he experience me? What am I in his world? I don't know. I may never know.

I keep singing. *Only you can look inside me.* . . .

Who will care for Matty when I am gone? Who will keep him safe? Or maybe I'll outlive him. Many children like Matthew don't live out a normal life span. Would it be better if he went first? As is often the case with Matty, I don't have the answers. What I do have, though, is this moment in the dark with him, his soft hand gently brushing my lips, the source of the soothing song, the same song he's heard nearly every night of his six years on the planet. Those hazel eyes of his which so seldom look into mine are easing shut.

Who am I, Lord, that you should know my name?

I finish the song and stand up and wonder what heaven will be for my son. Maybe it'll be a place a lot like here, a place where his own son will run from him across a wide-open field of green, every nerve-end in his little body singing, where afterwards, Matty and I can tip back a beer together at a pub. Where he has a healthy body and a lovely wife and our family can linger long over pasta and homemade bread and salad and red wine. Where his son, my grandson, will fall asleep in my lap, a sweaty load of spent boy pinning me to my chair on the deck, the night sounds stirring around us, the stars rioting in the dark sky.

I look down on Matty's peaceful sleeping face. So often peace has eluded him: the operations, the I.V.s, the straps tying his hands to the hospital bed rails so he wouldn't pull the needles out, the countless blood draws when they couldn't find the vein, all the insults descending out of the blue onto my little boy who couldn't understand why the people around him had suddenly begun torturing him. But he is at peace right now. And a time is coming when he will have peace and have it to the full. And all the other things he's been robbed of. Meeting a girl. Playing catch with his father and his son. Making love. Calling his mother's name aloud. Talking with his twin sister. Eating a pizza. Drinking a beer. Running. And I'll get to be there with him. God will carve out a little slice of eternity for us, our own private do-over where the breeze carries the smell of fresh-cut grass, where the sky is bluer than you ever thought it could be, where the air feels newborn.

Soon, Matty. Soon.

Bruce Lawrie is a writer in Moraga, California.

WORDS ARE NOT ENOUGH

ALICE LOK CAHANA

Alice Lok Cahana, imprisoned in Auschwitz as a teenager, spoke at the university one day, and no one will ever forget it.

I WANT TO TELL YOU the miracles that happened in Auschwitz. And the people who despised the Nazis and how they turned around from despising.

Here is one story. I met a man in Israel who told me: I was fourteen years old when the Nazis came into my house, and we had prayer exactly at that moment, and my father said: *Take the Torah and put it around your body and go out from the room.* And the boy went and did exactly what his father said. And he arrived to Auschwitz. In Auschwitz, first they undress you, he went up to one of the Polish people and he said, I cannot undress, I am carrying a Torah, the Torah is the most sacred book we have. The Polish man got scared and he went around saying the boy has a Torah on him, we cannot let him into the crematorium. Soon everyone surrounded the young man. They said to him, you cannot undress; pretend that you are finding some work in the clothing. Because people undress, they left their clothes on the ground, and then into the crematorium they go. The young SS soldier who was waiting outside the crematorium, he said to them, you must tell me what you are hiding, because all of you will die anyhow. And the young SS soldier found out that this little boy was carrying a Torah, and he went to the boy and said: Listen, I know what you are doing. Listen, every morning you come to me I will help you get food and you don't go to work. And guess what happened? This young man survived and the Torah survived, and it is in Jerusalem. The moment I heard that story I decided to create scrolls. I don't know how to do it but I want to celebrate the scrolls. The sanctity has to go with us no matter where we are. And so I made scrolls, and each one has a name, and I made one with that boy's name.

Here is another story. When I was in Auschwitz, I kept asking, why am I here, what did I do wrong? What did my grandfather do wrong? What did my father do wrong? And I decided I knew what we did wrong: *We read the letters backwards, that was our mistake.* The letters that always revived me! They killed us because we read the letters backwards! But after Auschwitz, when I read the Torah, the letters revive me again and again, so that could not be it. That could not be. And a young American man, he put me in the right knowledge. You didn't do nothing wrong, he said, the world did something wrong, terribly wrong. This young man, he went to Budapest in the beginning of it all, and he saved Jews, he gave out passports of Sweden, and because the Hungarians didn't know how to read Swedish, this was how my father was saved. And thousands of others too, with these pieces of paper. I am here to tell you that one man can make a difference, and that man can be you, any of you. Your task is to better the world.

I made a painting that has holes in it. Why is there holes? Because God says to us, I can not do all. I can create you, but I cannot do it all. You have to help Me fix the holes and put everything together. This is the learning from the Holocaust. That each of us is here to fix the holes. My little brother, they put him in the crematorium. What did my mother, undressing in front of strangers, holding this little boy by the hand, what did she say to him? What? No one knows. *There* is a hole.

You know everything was terrible in Auschwitz. There was no food, there was no water, there was cold, you didn't know whether your father or mother lives. I worked in a factory in Auschwitz. One day in the factory, it was almost Christmas, and the snow that fell was like a table set for guests, it was so beautiful, it was so white. And of course we had to work inside, starting at five o'clock in the morning and finishing at five o'clock at night, and not having food or anything we need. The foreman watching us every minute making sure we are making every ammunition supposed to be made. And the foreman looked at me and called me over. I was sure I was to be punished because all the way walking there the SS man is whipping his whip. You don't work fast and you don't do the work like it is supposed to, they beat you. I was fifteen years old and my legs are shaking. I am trying to tell him please just don't hurt me. Please I will work faster. And the foreman says bend down bend down bend down and I feel that he is about to be beating me he says take that white bread, put it under your coat, and go out fast. That was my Christmas. What an incredible man. The SS man was behind him. He bet his life to give a child a chance. You know what a slice of white bread meant? Could you imagine that I am starving? Instead of beating me he gave me bread I could share with my sister. So you see, everywhere there are good people, everywhere.

I don't know how much you know about the Holocaust. What is your interest in it? What do you want to do with your life, where do you want to go? What is hurting in you? What are your holes to fix? What is now important in my life, and in your life also, is that after the Holocaust, we shaking hands with each other, that we are nobody lesser than the other. That we understand the real meaning of what God created us for. You have the task. You have the task to better this world. There are holes in people also but those we create and we can fix with love. God wants us whole. We should fix the hole and make a good human being. Use all of your hands. One time I gave a painting to the pope, Pope Benedict. He said to me come, come!, and he held my hands. I tell him the painting is us arriving to Auschwitz, we were so frightened, and the first thing they did, they took away your name, so that you are not a person, you are a number. When you don't have name, you are nobody. The pope asks why is yellow in the painting and I tell him that is the yellow stain, that is the odor in Auschwitz, that odor never left me. That wonderful man had tears in his eyes. He held my hands for nineteen minutes. Then they put my painting by the Sistine Chapel.

My grandfather was a wonderful person and he said about the Nazis, it cannot happen in Hungary, maybe in Poland, maybe they didn't know, maybe, maybe, maybe, and we had all kind of maybes, you understand, and we didn't want to believe. Because just like you are sitting here, you would not believe. What, Germany? Germany is wonderful, they wouldn't do that. When I arrive to Auschwitz, I say to my sister, you know, somebody made a mistake. Very soon they will come and apologize. Somebody will apologize; we don't belong here. People running around in pajamas, what is this? Insane asylum, what is this? It cannot happen. We did not believe like you would not believe, you would not believe that it can happen in your town. We didn't believe. And unfortunately because we didn't believe, this is where we got.

In Auschwitz, there is a thousand people in a barrack, can you imagine that? In the barrack there is a bunk and six people are on it, nothing, no pillow, no cover, no nothing. Just one little piece of cloth, and if any of us wanted to turn on our side, the others had to turn to that side also. It was so cold, unbelievably cold. In the beginning, you know what I did? I gave away my bread. I say, I will not eat this, this is terrible bread! I got shiny brown shoes on me then, and somebody said they give sometimes a little margarine here, I said, margarine? We never had margarine, we ate butter, you know. And I put the margarine on my shoes, until I realize this is our food. So you slowly adapted yourself to something so horrendous that you cannot believe the human being can be like that, or do that to each other. So this is what we have to do, beautiful people, this is what we have to do: not to hate, not to hate, not ever.

Now you cannot imagine what it means to go out to freedom after Auschwitz. How do you go to freedom? How should I enter freedom? I did not even have a dress. I was sent to Sweden and someone invited me to Passover. Someone gave me a blue dress. I went to the door and I could not enter. I walked around in the flowers. Finally I went and opened the door, and it was beautiful halls and beautiful tables and people, you know, and the lady who invited me, she says, there is a little room there, why don't you just go and change? Ha, I didn't have anything to change into! But I went to the little room and saw a calendar and I said to myself, I will learn the days in English, and so I learned all the days until all the guests arrived. Finally everybody sat down, and they started to talk, and guess what they talked about? The price of the gold on the international market. And I thought, my god, this is how you celebrate the Passover? You know how many people were put in the crematorium a day? So very quietly I took my coat and walked down into Stockholm until I had no tears. I thought, what will I do with my freedom? Will I be quiet or will I scream? But it cannot happen again! At that time, I decided, I will not be silent. But of course my art is very silent, because some of the things you want to say, words are not enough, and only the art can talk.

I was very embarrassed what I did, very embarrassed. I thought if my mother would be alive she would never permit me to get up from any table and leave the house. And when I met my husband I said I have only one wish, take me back to Sweden so I can apologize this family for being so rude and leaving them, and my husband said, I do it for you. We went to Sweden back and I went to the same house and the lady say to me, I don't remember you. And my husband holding the flowers and I'm crying. So life is very interesting. Because you cannot expect everything. I had the task to tell you my story, and now I am eighty years old and it's very hard, because I am crying every day. Where is my brother, where is my mother, what happened to them? And so I have the task, nobody else. I have the task, no matter how hard it is, to come here, and tell you my story. I will tell you one more story: Steven Spielberg in his film about five of us who survived [*The Last Days*] did something colossal for me. I told him I will do what he asked me to do, go back to Auschwitz, but he has to do me one thing, he has to help me find my sister, this is 56 years after she dies. And guess what happens? The German person who was in charge of who died and who was alive opened the books, and here is my sister's name. And so after 56 years, I found my sister. My husband and I put down a stone for her and there she is under a tree and leaves cover the tree.

You know why I give the pope the painting? Because the first thing he did, when he became a pope, he went to Auschwitz and he kneeled and prayed and asked how could this happen? When I read that in the paper I thought to myself, this is it, I have to thank him somehow, because after all these years he could easily do nothing and be quiet. But he didn't.

How did I deal with God in Auschwitz? This is a very strange story. My sister Idit and I decided that we would pray every Friday for the Sabbath. But they didn't let us pray, they didn't let us speak. We had to be quiet. We had to be nothing. So one Friday night I say, why don't we pray inside the latrine? So we went to a corner in the latrine and started to pray, and the Hebrew songs, you know, are almost universal, and more children came, from all over the world it was people there, and the children heard us praying in Hebrew and singing, and for a moment, a moment, God was with us there, and we all prayed, and every week, more and more people prayed. We discovered that the SS would not go into this filthy place. So this is where we prayed. And it is also very beautiful thing of Steven Spielberg, when I went back to Auschwitz, I saw the latrine still there, and I started to scream, and he says what are you talking about? So I told him the story, and he got some Jewish boys to sing the same songs in the latrine, if you listen carefully you will hear them, young children singing. The song they sang means, *Angels who come here, bless these children, bless them and bless the world.*

Here is one more story. When they took us from our home they put us in a cattle train and there was two buckets there, one with water for drinking and the other for sanitary use. There were eighty people in the train, men and women and a woman who was pregnant. Idit and I could not bear to use the bucket in the corner. So when we got to the border there was a young soldier who opened the door for fresh air. I said to him, please please let me go down for a minute under the wheels, my sister and I cannot bear to going to the bathroom in the bucket. And he understood and let me down. Wasn't it a miracle?

Alice Lok Cahana is an artist who lives in Houston, Texas. The quietest, smilingest lady you ever saw. How could she not be bitter? And yet she is not bitter. There are many teachers.

HER

On a dream coming beautifully true.

BILL MCNAMARA

OUR ROMANCE BEGAN in the 1930s, long before she even knew it, with a garden, a hedge, and a wall of silence between us. She was on the sandlot side of the hedge, taking a shortcut home from junior high. I didn't have to make a date or set a clock; every weekday when she and her school chums approached my line of vision from a kitchen window where I sat with a peanut-butter sandwich and a glass of milk, my head would just swivel due west as though a cranium magnet was drifting by. After which, head and heart swimming like goldfish, I would repair to the outdoors—rendered empty in her wake—to peddle my afternoon papers.

At the time, of course, she was blissfully unaware of the bombs bursting in the air, of the dreams that empowered me to know the gentleness of her touch and the timbre of her voice, though I had no clue, sad to say, as to how I might advance the inevitable. I was at that time scared silly of girls and yet, for someone so seismically smitten, remarkably patient.

Two years went by, not exactly flying. On a somber Saturday evening my sister Rita, in desperation mode, asked me to take her to the Policemen's Ball. She was holding two tickets—not to mention her breath—anticipating a *What are you, nuts?* But, no, this once I did the noble thing: I caved.

We sat near the dance floor, enjoying the big-band music and digging the terpsichorean moves of the more seasoned couples. A new set was under way and couples were descending from the tiered seats aft. A sweet voice belonging to one of the descenders caressed my ears: *O look, there's my friend Rita!* Then, a few decibels higher but sweet still:

hi Ri! My sister, being Ri, turned in response while I sat rigid, struck dumb by an epiphany of sorts.

The voice I'd heard only in my sleep was gliding down the steps upon which my left foot was numbly resting. And yes, Mr. Ripley, it was the dream come true. We met. She smiled. Smiles to set your heart dancing. Radiance to make your eyes blink. Beauty to bend your knees. Composure to render you speechless and duly rendered was I. She was a classmate of Rita's. Her name was Kay. Still is. Her surname, Peterson, was parenthesized in 1944 to make room for McNamara. On one of our dates, she mentioned that her big wish was to be married young and have five sons. Done and done. And the five sons begat fifteen grandchildren who in turn begat ten great-grandchildren, so far. Meanwhile, the aleatory bloke chosen to be accessory to these signs and wonders stands by in stunned but grateful silence, trying like the dickens to remember all their names.

Bill McNamara is a writer in Rhode Island.

A WAR STORY

In the middle of Iraq in the middle of a war,
there was a moment. . . .

PETE ROOKS

WE CROSSED INTO IRAQ in late March. We were the Bastogne Brigade, so named because we held Bastogne in the Second World War. I was a major. We had 700 people and 350 pieces of rolling stock and we went through Basra, where we got a fairly good reception, and through Nazaria, where we got some mortars and grenades and snipers. That was standard fare. That was the way it was.

We stopped just south of Najaf. The city is up on a bluff. One of the holiest cities in Shi'a Islam. The founder of Shi'a is said to be buried there. Noah and Adam and Eve are said to be buried there. Some say it was the Garden of Eden. We want to get to the Golden Dome, the Imam Ali Mosque, to talk to the current imam, Ayatolla Ali Sistani, who had been imprisoned by Saddam Hussein.

But this is a war and we can't just wander in.

We send infantry in and we discover we are no longer fighting the uniformed forces of Iraq. They have faded into the population. Next morning we send in serious force. Our colonel leads the attack. I coordinate air strikes. Infantry sets up in the city in a girls' school. That night a frog missile lands near our base and we get moving and in the morning we are all in the city and we get ready to visit the mosque.

Bravo Company sets off for the mosque. We have about 130 people on foot. Ages seventeen to late forties. It was hot. The whole city is in the streets. Kids everywhere. You could smell cooking oil and dirt and dust and rubble and burnt cars. Kids were running alongside us and shouting *America good!* and *George Bush good!* This was early in the war and they were happy to be done with Saddam. Everyone seemed happy. But you're never comfortable in a war. Anything can happen any time. I am walking in the middle of the pack, yelling *stay focused! secure your stuff! head on a swivel! weapons up! scan your area!* There are hundreds of people all ages walking with us now. We're walking fast. We're in road march formation, staggered two by two, five meters apart, *stay focused!* We're moving briskly. Any time you stop or get separated you die. There are a lot of kids running with us. They had never seen Americans before. I saw little kids running alongside and I thought of my son who was not yet two at that time. Your mind drifts a little in a situation like that. You think, am I really doing this? I keep yelling. *Head on a swivel! weapons up!* I may have used bad language.

We go through the streets. Right turn, left turn, right turn, there's the mosque. There's a *sea* of people there and they're angry. They're afraid we're going to blow the mosque. The street is *packed*. We're in full gear, rifles and pistols and goggles and anti-tank weapons. We have a linguist with a bullhorn and she is shouting in Arabic that we are here in peace! we are here with respect! we are here to see the imam! we are here in peace! but the crowd isn't buying. Our colonel points his rifle down to indicate we are not here for war. Nothing. Then he orders us to take a knee and smile. Everyone goes down on one knee and smiles. The kids who were running with us take a knee and smile too. They're right in among us. And this actually works. Things calm down a little. Some rocks get thrown but no one gets shot. Things work out and we go back to base and that's the end of the story.

Could we have forced our way in? Absolutely.

But we used the biggest weapon, the one inside your helmet.

After Najaf we went on to Hillah, where we saw Daniel's lion's den, and where we tried to fix the schools and water pipes, and then on to Mosul, and a lot of us ended our tours there. I remember everything from the war except what I chose to forget. But I remember that morning in Najaf clear as day. It's a good story. People should hear that story. Somehow that story matters. Somehow it matters a lot.

Pete Rooks, who retired from the U.S. Army as a lieutenant colonel after 21 years of service, commanded the University's Army cadets from 2005 to 2009.

The Call to Forgiveness at the End of the Day

KATHLEEN DEAN MOORE

May 25, 2025. All those years, the Swainson's thrushes were the first to call in the mornings. Their songs spiraled like mist from the swale to the pink sky. That's when I would take a cup of tea and walk into the meadow. Swallows sat on the highest perches, whispering as they waited for light to stream onto the pond. Then they sailed through the midges, scattering motes of wing-light. Chipping sparrows buzzed like sewing machines as soon as the sun lit the Douglas firs. If I kissed the knuckle of my thumb, they came closer and trilled again.

For years there were flocks of goldfinches. After my husband and I poisoned the bull-thistles on the far side of the pond, the goldfinches perched in the willows. When they landed there, dew shook from the branches into the pond, throwing light into new leaves where chick-adees chirped. The garbage truck backed down the lane, beeping its backup call, making the frogs sing, even in the day.

Oh, there was music in the mornings, all those years. In the overture to the day, each bird added its call until the morning was an ecstasy of music that faded only when the diesel pumps kicked on to pull water from the stream to the neighbor's bing-cherry trees.

Evenings were glorious too. Just as the sun set, little brown bats began to fly. If a bat swooped close, I heard its tiny sonar chirps, just at the highest reach of my hearing. Each downward flitter of its wings squeezed its lungs and pumped out another chirp, the way a pump-organ exhales Bach. Frogs sang and sang, but not like bats or birds.

Like violins, violin strings just touched by the bow, the bow touching and withdrawing. They sang all evening, thousands of violins, and into the night. They sang while crows flew into the oaks and settled their wings, while garter snakes, their stomachs extended with frogs, crawled finally under the fallen bark of the oaks and stretched their lengths against cold ground.

I don't know how many frogs there were in the pond then. Thousands. Tens of thousands. Clumps of eggs like eyeballs in aspic. Neighborhood children poked them with sticks to watch their jelly shake. When the eggs hatched, there were tadpoles. I have seen the shallow edge of the pond black with wiggling tadpoles. There were that many, each with a song growing inside it and tiny black legs poking out behind. Just at dusk, a hooded merganser would sweep over the water, or a pair of geese, silencing the frogs. Then it was the violins again, and geese muttering.

In the years when the frog choruses began to fade, scientists said it was a fungus, or maybe bullfrogs were eating the tadpoles. No one knew what to do about the fungus, but people tried to stop the bullfrogs. Standing on the dike, my neighbor shot frogs with a pellet gun, embedding silver BBs in their heads, a dozen holes, until she said *how many holes can I make in a frog's face before it dies? Give me something more powerful.* So she took a shotgun and filled the bullfrogs with buckshot until, legs snapped, faces caved in, they slowly sank away. Ravens belled from the top of the oak.

When the bats stopped coming, they said that was a fungus too. When the goldfinches came in pairs, not flocks, we told each other the flocks must be feeding in a neighbor's field. No one could guess where the thrushes had gone.

Two springs later, there were drifts of tiny white skins scattered in the shallows like dust rags in the dusk. I scooped one up with a stick. It was a frog skin, a perfect empty sack, white, intact, but with no frog inside—cleaned, I supposed, by snails or winter—and not just one. Empty frogs scattered on the muddy bottom of the pond. They were as empty as the perfect emptiness of a bell, the perfectly shaped absence ringing the angelus, the evening song, the call for forgiveness at the end of the day.

As it happened, that was the spring when our granddaughter was born. I brought her to the pond so she could feel the comfort I had known there for so many years. Killdeer waddled in the mud by the shore, but even then, not so many as before. By then, the pond had sunk into its warm, weedy places, leaving an expanse of cracked earth. Ahead of the coming heat, butterflies fed in the mud between the cracks, unrolling their tongues to touch salty soil.

I held my granddaughter in my arms and sang to her then, an old lullaby that made her soften like wax in a flame, molding her little body to my bones. *Hush a bye, don't you cry. Go to sleep you little baby. Birds and the butterflies, fly through the land.* I held her close, weighing the chances of the birds and the butterflies. She fell asleep in my arms, unafraid.

I will tell you, I was so afraid.

Poets warned us, writing of the *heart-breaking beauty that will remain when there is no heart to break for it.* But what if it is worse than that? What if it's the heartbroken children who remain in a world without beauty? How will they find solace in a world without wild music? How will they thrive without green hills edged with oaks? How will they forgive us for letting frog-song slip away? When my granddaughter looks back at me, I will be on my knees, begging her to say I did all I could.

I didn't do all I could have done.

It isn't enough to love a child and wish her well. It isn't enough to open my heart to a bird-graced morning. Can I claim to love a morning, if I don't protect what creates its beauty? Can I claim to love a child, if I don't use all the power of my beating heart to preserve a world that nourishes children's joy? Loving is not a kind of *la-de-da.* Loving is a sacred trust. To love is to affirm the absolute worth of what you love and to pledge your life to its thriving—to protect it fiercely and faithfully, for all time.

Ring the angelus for the thrushes and the swallows. Ring the bells for frogs floating in bent reeds. Ring the bells for all of us who did not save the songs. Holy Mary, Mother of God, ring the bells for every sacred emptiness. Let them echo in the silence at the end of the day.

Forgiveness is too much to ask. I would pray for only this: that our granddaughter would hear again the little lick of music, that grace note toward the end of a meadowlark's song.

Meadowlarks. There were meadowlarks. They sang like angels in the morning.

Kathleen Dean Moore is the author of the superb essay collections Riverwalking *and* Holdfast, *and the editor of* Moral Ground: Ethical Action for a Planet in Peril. *See moralground.com.*

A CHAPEL IS WHERE
YOU CAN HEAR SOMETHING BEATING
BELOW YOUR HEART

I came to the chapel at the University
as the light was falling. . . .

Pico Iyer

GIANT FIGURES ARE TALKING and strutting and singing on enormous screens above me, and someone is chattering away on the mini-screen in the cab from which I just stepped. Nine people at this street corner are shouting into thin air, wearing wires around their chins and jabbing at screens in their hands. One teenager in Sacramento, I read recently, sent 300,000 text messages in a month—or ten a minute for every minute of her waking day, assuming she was awake sixteen hours a day. There are more cell-phones than people on the planet now, almost (ten mobiles for every one at the beginning of the century). Even by the end of the last century, the average human being in a country such as ours saw as many images in a day as a Victorian inhaled in a lifetime.

And then I walk off crowded Fifth Avenue and into the capacious silence of St. Patrick's. Candles are flickering here and there, intensifying my sense of all I cannot see. Figures are on their knees, heads bowed, drawing my attention to what cannot be said. Light is flooding through the great blue windows, and I have entered a realm where no I or realm exists. I notice everything around me: the worn stones, the little crosses, the hymn-books, the side chapels; then I sit down, close my eyes—and step out of time, into everything that stretches beyond it.

When I look back on my life, the parts that matter and sustain me, all I see is a series of chapels. They may be old or young, cracked brown or open space; they may be lectories or afterthoughts, hidden corners of a city or deserted spaces in the forest. They are as variable as people. But like people they have a stillness at the core of them which makes all discussion of high and low, East and West, you and me dissolve. Bells toll and toll and I lose all sense of whether they are chiming within me or without.

The first time I was asked to enter a New York office building—for a job interview twenty-eight years ago—I gathered myself, in all senses, in St. Patrick's, and knew that it would put everything I was about to face (a company, a new life, my twittering ambitions) into place. It was the frame that gave everything else definition. Ever since, I've made it my practice to step into that great thronged space whenever I return to the city, to remind myself of what is real, what is lasting, before giving myself to everything that isn't. A chapel is the biggest immensity we face in our daily lives, unless we live in a desert or in the vicinity of the Grand Canyon. A chapel is the deepest silence we can absorb, unless we stay in a cloister. A chapel is where we allow ourselves to be broken open as if we were children again, trembling at home before our parents.

Whenever I fly, I step into an airport chapel. The people there may be sleeping, reading, praying, but all of them are there because they want to be collected. When I go to San Francisco, I stay across from Grace Cathedral, and visit it several times a day, to put solid ground underneath my feet. Returning to the college I attended, I sit on a pew at the back, listening to the high-voiced choir, and think back on that shuffling kid who wandered the downy grounds and what relation he might have to the person who now sits here.

So much of our time is spent running from ourselves, or hiding from the world; a chapel brings us back to the source, in ourselves and in the larger sense of self—as if there were a difference. Look around you. Occasional figures are exploring their separate silences; the rich and the poor are hard to tell apart, with heads bowed. Light is diffused and general; when you hear voices, they are joined in a chorus or reading from a holy book. The space at the heart of the Rothko Chapel is empty, and that emptiness is prayer and surrender.

In 1929 the British Broadcasting Corporation decided to start broadcasting "live silence" in memory of the dead instead of just halting transmission for two minutes every day; it was important, it was felt, to hear the rustle of papers, the singing of birds outside, an occasional cough. As a BBC spokesman put it, with rare wisdom, silence is "a solvent which destroys personality and gives us leave to be great and universal." Permits us, in short, to be who we are and could be if only we had the openness and trust. A chapel is where we hear something and nothing, ourselves and everyone else, a silence that is not the absence of noise but the presence of something much deeper: the depth beneath our thoughts.

This spring I came, for the first time, to the Chapel of Christ the Teacher at the University of Portland, to give a talk as the light was falling. Great shafts of sunshine stretched across the courtyard, catching and sharpening the faces of students returning to their rooms. Later in the evening, since this was Holy Week, an enormous cross was carried into the space, in darkness and reverence and silence. Now, however, people were walking in from all directions, leaving themselves at the door, putting away their business cards and gathering in a circle. They said nothing, and looked around them. The light through the windows began to fade. A scatter of seats became a congregation. And whatever was said, or not said, became less important than the silence.

Many years ago, when I was too young to know better, I worked in a 25th-floor office four blocks from Times Square, in New York City. Teletypes juddered the news furiously into our midst every second—this was the World Affairs department of *Time* magazine—and messengers breathlessly brought the latest reports from our correspondents to our offices. Editors barked, early computers sputtered, televisions in our senior editors' offices gave us the news as it was breaking. We spoke and conferred and checked facts and wrote, often, twenty or twenty-five pages in an evening.

I left all that for a monastery on the backstreets of Kyoto. I wanted to learn about silence. I wanted to learn about who I was when I wasn't thinking about it. The Japanese are masters of not saying anything, both because their attention is always on listening, on saying little, even on speaking generically, and because, when they do talk, they are very eager to say nothing offensive, outrageous, or confrontational. They're like talk-show hosts in a nation where self-display is almost forbidden. You learn more by listening than talking, they know; you create a wider circle not by thinking about yourself, but about the people around you, and how you can find common ground with them. The Japanese idea of a dream date—I've been with my Japanese sweetheart for 23 years and now I know—is to go to a movie and come out saying nothing.

Perhaps I wouldn't need this kind of training in paying attention and keeping quiet were it not for the fact that I used to love babbling, and my colleges and friends in England and the U.S. trained and encouraged me to talk, to thrust myself forward, to assert my little self in all its puny glory. Perhaps we wouldn't need chapels if our lives were already clear and calm (a saint or a Jesus may never need to go into a church; he's always carrying one inside himself). Chapels are emergency rooms for the soul. They are the one place we can reliably go to find who we are and what we should be doing with our lives—usually by finding all we aren't, and what is much greater than us, to which we can only give ourselves up.

"I like the silent church," Emerson wrote, "before the service begins."

I grew up in chapels, at school in England. For all the years of my growing up, we had to go to chapel every morning and to say prayers in a smaller room every evening. Chapel became everything we longed to flee; it was where we made faces at one another, doodled in our hymnbooks, sniggered at each other every time we sang about "the bosom of the Lord" or the "breast" of a green hill. All we wanted was open space, mobility, freedom—the California of the soul. But as the years went on, I started to see that no movement made sense unless it had a changelessness beneath it; that all our explorations were only as rich as the still place we brought them back to.

I noticed, in my early thirties, that I had accumulated 1.5 million miles with United Airlines alone; I started going to a monastery. It wasn't in order to become religious or to attend services in the chapel, though I did go there, over and over, as Emerson might have done, when nobody was present. The real chapel was my little cell at the monastery, looking out on the boundless blue of the Pacific Ocean below, the Steller's jay that just alighted on the splintered fence in my garden. Chapel was silence and spaciousness and whatever put the human round, my human, all too human thoughts, in some kind of vaster context.

My house had burned down eight months before, and kind friends might have been thinking that I was seeking out a home; but in the chapel of my cell, I was seeking only a reminder of the inner home we always carry with us. To be a journalist is to be beholden to the contents of just now, the news, the public need; to be a human—even if you're a journalist—is to be conscious of the old, what stands outside of time, our prime necessity. I could only write for *Time*, I thought, if I focused on Eternity.

I've stayed in those little cells in a Benedictine hermitage above the sea more than fifty times by now, over almost twenty years. I've stayed in the cloister with the monks; spent three weeks at a time in silence; stayed in a trailer in the dark, and in a house for the monastery's laborers, where I'd come upon monks doing press-ups against the rafters on the ground floor and planning their next raid upon the monastery computer.

Now the place lives inside me so powerfully that my home in Japan looks and feels like a Benedictine hermitage. I receive no newspapers or magazines there, and I watch no television. I've never had a cell-phone, and I've ensured that we have almost no Internet connections at all. We have no car or bicycle, and the whole apartment (formerly, population four, my wife and two children and myself) consists of two rooms. I sleep on a couch in the living room at 8:30 every night, and think this is the most luxurious, expansive, liberating adventure I could imagine.

A chapel is where you can hear something beating below your heart.

We've always needed chapels, howsever confused or contradictory we may be in the way we define our religious affiliations; we've always had to have quietness and stillness to undertake our journeys into battle, or just the tumult of the world. How can we act in the world, if we haven't had the time and chance to find out who we are and what the world and action might be?

But now Times Square is with us everywhere. The whole world is clamoring at our door even on a mountaintop (my monastery has wireless Internet, its workers downloaded so much of the world recently that the system crashed, and the monastery has an electric address, www.contemplation.com). Even in my cell in Japan, I can feel more than 6 billion voices, plus the Library of Alexandria, CNN, MSNBC, everything, in that inoffensive little white box with the apple on it. Take a bite, and you fall into the realm of Knowledge, and Ignorance, and Division.

The high-tech firm Intel experimented for seven months with enforcing "Quiet Time" for all of its workers for at least four consecutive hours a week (no e-mails were allowed, no phone calls accepted). It tried banning all e-mail checks on Fridays and assuring its workers that they had 24 hours, not 24 minutes, in which to respond to any internal e-mail. If people are always running to catch up, they will never have the time and space to create a world worth catching up with. Some colleges have now instituted a vespers hour, though often without a church; even in the most secular framework, what people require is the quietness to sink beneath the rush of the brain. Journalist friends of mine switch off their modems from Friday evening to Monday morning, every week, and I am enviously admiring; I know that when I hop around the Web, watch YouTube videos, surf the TV set, I turn away and feel agitated. I go for a walk, enjoy a real conversation with a friend, turn off the lights and listen to Bach or Leonard Cohen, and I feel palpably richer, deeper, fuller, happier.

Happiness is absorption, being entirely yourself and entirely in one place. That is the chapel that we crave.

Long after my home had burned down, and I had begun going four times a year to my monastery up the coast, long after I'd constructed a more or less unplugged life in Japan—figuring that a journalist could write about the news best by not following its every convulsion, and writing from the chapel and not the madness of Times Square—I found a Christian retreat-house in my own hometown. Sometimes, when I had an hour free in the day, or was running from errand to errand, I drove up into the silent hills and parked there, and just sat for a few minutes in its garden. Encircled by flowers. In a slice of light next to a statue of the Virgin.

Instantly, everything was okay. I had more reassurance than I would ever need. I was thinking of something more than an "I" I could never entirely respect.

Later, I opened the heavy doors and walked into the chapel, again when no one was there. It sat next to a sunlit courtyard overlooking the dry hills and far-off blue ocean of what could have been a space in Andalusia. A heavy bell spoke of the church's private sense of time. A row of blond-wood chairs was gathered in a circle. I knelt and closed my eyes and thought of the candle flickering in one corner of the chapel I loved in the monastery up the coast.

When I had to go to Sri Lanka, in the midst of its civil war, I went to the chapel to be still; to gather my resources and protection, as it were. I went there when I was forcibly evacuated from the house that my family had rebuilt after our earlier structure had burned down, and our new home was surrounded by wild flames driven by seventy-mile-per-hour winds. In the very same week, my monastery in Big Sur was also encircled by fire.

I went there even when I was halfway across the world, because I had reconstituted the chapel in my head, my heart; it was where I went to be held by something profound. Then another wildfire struck up, and a newspaper editor called me in Japan: my retreat-house near my home was gone.

Where does one go when one's chapel is reduced to ash? Perhaps it is the first and main question before us all. There are still chapels everywhere. And I go to them. But like the best of teachers or friends, they always have the gift of making themselves immaterial, invisible—even, perhaps, immortal. I sit in Nara, the capital of Japan twelve centuries ago, and I see a candle flickering. I feel the light descending from a skylight in the rotunda roof. I hear a fountain in the courtyard. I close my eyes and sit very still, by the side of my bed, and sense the chapel take shape around me.

If your silence is deep enough, bells toll all the way through it.

Pico Iyer is the author of many books, including The Open Road: The Global Journey of the Fourteenth Dalai Lama.

THE HOPE OF A TRAIL

*"For all I know I am approaching
the holiest place in the world. Who can say?
Who knows? We know nothing. . . ."*

RICK BASS

THE PEACE RIVER runs east as it leaves the mountains of British Columbia, and travels in lazy, powerful curves across the plains, toward the Arctic Ocean, some thousand miles away. Within the mile-wide canyon of the river's hidden valley, there are groves of aspen, spruce, pine, and fields in which farmers grow hay, ranchers raise cattle, and gardeners grow immense crops of berries, carrots, peaches, lettuce. The Peace River valley contains the richest soil in Canada, courtesy of each spring's flooding, which deposited rich silt for thousands of years before two dams were built here. Now a third dam is proposed, the false lake of which will cover the land, long the ancestral home of the West Moberley tribe, where deer, elk, bears, cougars, lynx, moose, and a hundred hardy families live.

To place another dam here—to drown this valley in still more slackwater—would be to kill the wildness that remains, and to foment yet more drilling rigs, pavement, manic boomtown construction frenzy, cranes, mobile homes, and pumpjacks.

It's not just animal and human histories that will be buried forever by a third dam. Already, the first two dams have submerged untold sites of pristine dinosaur track fossils of hadrosaurs and ichthyosaurs, remains of First Nation encampments, and petroglyph sites. Toxic metals are accumulating in the two false lakes, and wells and drinking water are already compromised by rising mercury levels in the sinks of the stagnant and unnatural waters.

Drown the river and the wild heart of the valley dies.

Today I am climbing to a tiny patch in the forest where long ago an underground seam of coal ignited, and still burns. The explorer Alexander Mackenzie wrote about it in his journals. It's a small place in the woods, a friend tells me, about the size of the kitchen area in an urban apartment, on a steep cliff high above the second of the false lakes.

I walk beneath a massive twin set of transcontinental power lines, which crackle, buzz, and sputter just above me, the unending angry hornet's-nest of our ceaseless demands for power. Cattle have been grazing in the cleared area just beneath the power lines, but all else is dense and dripping lovely green forest. For a while, I walk in the woods, to spare my tender brain the uninterrupted close-range reception of radio waves transmitted by the pulsing surge above, and also to be out of the steady downpour, but progress is too slow, and I come back out of the leafy woods and plod in the steady downpour through the grasses cow-gnawed as short as the grass on a putting green.

According to my friend's hand-drawn map (on a napkin, the very best kind of map), I am to follow a wild little creek into the forest before finding a faint game trail that bends east. The creek's there, but what does he mean by a trail? A thin space between trees? A game path? He had suggested it might be difficult to discern, which, coming from him, could very well mean I'm looking for blades of grass bent only that morning by the passing of a fawn. An indecipherable wisp, the *possibility* of a trail.

I proceed on faith.

And to my delight I find a tiny, tiny trail, so overgrown with grass that it would be easy for anyone to call it only a continuation of more forest, more growth. But it is definitely a lessening in the growth, a subtle crease in the vegetative uproar, one which, after an hour of bushwhacking, presents itself to me not so much like a trail but like a thought half-formed, or a memory from childhood, buried beneath years of accumulated detritus. It is as if I have pushed blindly into the deep forest only to find this possibility, this *hope* of a trail.

I walk farther. The trail is stippled here and there with the pellets of deer and elk. The forest is thinning. I enter an aspen grove, where the stark white bark is limned with toothmarks from elk and moose and the curved clawmark-hieroglyphics of bears.

I reach the edge of a cliff, and far down below me is the dam, and the slender green lake it made, covering a secret world now obscured from us, seemingly gone forever. It was only yesterday, in a sense, that Mackenzie and his companions brought their canoes up over the terrible, beautiful waterfall that blocked their path there, where the dam now squats; although one distant day the dam will crumble and be gone, and the waterfall that lies buried will be revealed again.

I pass through another aspen grove, with bunchberry dogwood and paintbrush in full bloom, and suddenly find my quarry in front of me: a modest little garden-sized patch of steam rising from bare soil, like the remains of a campfire from the night before. I can smell the slightest tang of sulfur. I am unsure whether I should approach the spot, feeling somehow that I shouldn't, that some respect is to be accorded, so I crouch and watch it burn, as it has been burning for perhaps thousands of years.

There are no flames and yet it burns. It is no fire lit by man. It may have been lit before there was such a thing as man.

I'm glad the steam vent wasn't submerged when the second dam was built. I'm glad there's no clear trail to this place, glad a secret place exists here in the violent and beautiful mountains.

I walk carefully toward the vent; for all I know the crust of the earth here has thinned from the ceaseless burning, and I might fall through and be reabsorbed into the fires of the earth, never to be heard from again. For all I know I am approaching the holiest place in the world. Who can say? Who knows? We know nothing.

At the edge of it I notice a small circle of rocks, smooth stones sunk now nearly beneath the surface, encrusted with black lichens. Someone placed these rocks here, a long time ago. Someone came here for visions and quests, for spiritual purposes perhaps.

I back away out of respect. I am of a place and time that needs so much, uses so much, expects so much, that my tribe has dammed the valley below and the valley above, and now we are coming after the next one, and I suppose the one after that, and the next. It's nothing more than chance that this little spot was not erased.

I stand silently by this holy place, and imagine the kind of men and women who used to come here, across the millennia. The way they approached was surely nothing like the way I came: I walked among cow-patties, beneath the hissing electricity of power lines. They walked through the ancient silence.

There is the profane and there is the sacred.

A long time ago something lit a fire here, and it has been burning ever since. Surely, at the very least, we are still capable, in our profanity, of witnessing the sacred, and protecting it, and preserving it beyond our hungry reach. Surely we are capable of that. Are we capable of that?

Rick Bass is the author of many books of fiction and non-, among them the sweet and piercing Colter.

When I Was Blind
"Blindness was full of second sight. . . ."

Edward Hoagland

I WAS BLIND for a while, and walking in the woods was an adventure. The white bark of birch trees beckoned to me. I would stroll through cushiony dead poplar leaves or fountaining ferns like ostrich plumes as high as my chest. I could hear squirrels quarreling and veerys veerying. Wood sorrel grew underfoot, the leaves tart when you taste them. Bears fattened on beechnuts in the fall up here and pitcher plants and orchids could be found in a kind of suspended bog.

When I was blind I listened to the radio scanner chatter softly, pulling in transmissions from the State Police, the Sheriff's Department, the Border Patrol, the town Rescue Squad, and the hospital at the county seat. You could also hear several fire departments, the Fish and Game frequency that wardens called in on, the Civil Air Patrol, railroad dispatchers, and various ham channels that lonely civilians talked on. You might hear EMT personnel resuscitate a heart patient, panting over him on air; or a fire in progress, actually even crackling; or a cop chasing a car thief through the woods, but mostly highway crews gabbing with headquarters interminably.

My neighbor trapped fisher, fox, and beaver in the swamp in season, shot venison, caught catfish, logged pulpwood, knew where the otters denned and the herons nested, where snappers could be dug out for a turtle stew, where a patch of lady's-slippers flourished where any girl might pick a moccasin-flower for her prom. But he had medical bills, and no money laid aside till his social security kicked in, so he was a junkyard watchman for money. The man who owned the junkyard was a war veteran too, and both men knew the old bootlegger paths through the swamp. The swamp was eight miles wide, and you could make a living limbing cedar trees and dragging them out for post-and-rail fencing or patio furniture, or from saw-log cherry wood or yellow birch and bird's-eye maple in the higher spots. Japanese businessmen owned the swamp now, having bought it from Wall Street investors, who had bought it from the logging company who had worked it over when everybody was young. The logging company had employed the county's jailbirds to cut tamaracks for telephone poles, plus any local who wanted to slug it out with the trees, hauling with horses as often as not, because of the braided streams. It was a good life until you broke a leg or got a rupture, and the logging led you into necks of the woods where nobody had trapped lately and you might nab a sixty-dollar bobcat overnight, half a month's pay.

When you are blind you can hear people smile—there's a soft click when their lips part. Once I went to see a healer in the woods. "Ease up on milk and Tums. Are you centered with the Lord? Do you tithe? Are you asking Him for guidance? Is your daughter in trouble? I have patients who fall out of bed every night, their dreams are so bad. Smoke much? Lemme see your nails. Chew your nails? You pray? Farm paid for? Be tremulous before the Lord! I'll pray for you, if you wish. But you wouldn't want me spitting into your eyes, like Jesus did with the blind man. Am I right? Praise the Lord. Eat less. Un-quietness eats at you. Stand underneath God. Get under His spotlight. No charge."

It used to be that the way you milked cows was you strapped a milking stool to your butt and wore it like a stiff set of bug's legs sticking out for half the day. No more. In the old days here, before the economics of farming forced you to trundle each cow off to be ground into hamburger once her most productive years were past, you'd become friends with your cows, and you felt an intimacy with the personalities of each, milking by hand, not machine. Although you shot every hawk or owl you saw, you treated your cows better then.

When I was blind I loved to ride trains, to sit in the Observation Car and chat with strangers, or in the dining car, the club car. When you can't see, age is less of a factor, no skin tone or paunchy posture to go by. Voices wrinkle later than faces, and, emanating from inside, seem truer to the nature residing there, harder to educate in concealment or deceit. Voices register compassion, disdain, apprehension, confidence, or surprise more directly, if you've learned to listen.

Rain squalls wet the spiders' webs just enough to glisten so that I could see them, though trees remained a bit of a puzzle, like shapes viewed underwater. But I could hear better—the giggle of the flying loons, rattle of a kingfisher, a hermit thrush seeking an answer from distant softwoods, the passage of a large milk snake through the stone wall where it ate chipmunks.

Another neighbor, who worked at the sawmill, had taught his dog to snatch food scraps out of the air when he, the neighbor, was having lunch and tossed them. But one day two of his fingers were sliced off by the saw and flew through the air and the dog caught and ate them. *So I'm a part of him now for as long as he lives,* said the guy.

When your sight evaporates, your forehead seems to lower incrementally, appropriating the area formerly occupied by the eyes. Thus more brain space is created—as well as more time to think. You hope.

Offered for auction today in town: cows, a llama, a guitar, a hare, a truck tire, a wheelchair. Who died? *Play it safe*, says the auctioneer, *you'll never get one cheaper when you need it.* Afterwards the cashier puts a bottle of whiskey on the counter, signaling the end of the auction and a drink for everyone with money for a poker game.

Blindness was full of second sight. I saw how the money economy had failed my neighbors after a lifetime of busy days, a web of energetic routines. Their house insurance had lapsed, the property tax bill was a yearly -ordeal, but social security hadn't yet kicked in. So fragile, though surges of mercy in other people did bubble up.

Edward Hoagland is the author of twenty books of essays, travel, and fiction, among them the Northwest classic Notes from the Century Before.

WHY I AM A PRIEST

Father Charles Gordon, C.S.C.

I LOVE BEING A PRIEST for all the usual reasons, which are excellent, and I revere them, but here are some other reasons.

I love being a priest because it is great to be something that has been around so long that it is practically hard-wired into the human brain. There have probably been people recognizable as priests about as long as there have been people recognizable as people. If a guy wandered out of the Pleistocene epoch and into a church and saw me behind the altar he'd likely have a pretty good idea what I was and what I was doing. And if Origen of Alexandria or Theodore of Mopsuestia or Eleanor of Aquitaine or Shakespeare of Avon or Shakespeare's tailor walked into the church they would know exactly what I was and exactly what I was doing. This matters to me because I'm a romantic by nature and find it moving to think about. More importantly, because a priest is such an ancient thing to be, an encounter with one touches very deep chords in the human mind and heart. Strains of longing, hope, and dread are sounded, as are any number of other feelings, some for which there are not yet names, and doubtless some for which the names have been forgotten. They are feelings as old and profound as those stirred by an encounter with a solar eclipse or a virgin queen.

Once you are known to be a priest you are treated differently. Walk through an airport in clerical dress: a stranger might pull you aside and pour out a story of joy, grief, or repentance; and moments later you might receive from another passerby a glance of such unfathomable loathing that it makes you miss a step. Despite the unpleasant aspects, the thing I love about all this is that my meetings with other people are freighted with possibility. The energy is there, at some level, for almost anything to happen. And God willing, what happens might be full of grace.

I love being a priest because right now there are more than a billion people in the world for whom I'm not only a priest but also their priest. On the off chance that we ever meet, they will know what to make of me, and I will have a way to be with them.

I love being a priest because I hear about miracles. Many people think miracles don't happen, or are very rare, but this is only because people tend not to tell each other about their miracles. But they'll tell a priest.

I know a woman who was comforted by an angel and a man who was visited by the Blessed Virgin Mary. I know a woman whose beloved father died when she was barely out of her teens. When it happened, she turned to the scriptures for solace. She opened her Bible at random and read, "In place of your fathers will be your sons." She was single then. Now she is married and has four children, all of them boys. That is her miracle.

And then there are the conversion stories. I know a fellow who when he was a graduate student was teetering on the brink of faith. One night, while walking past the darkened shop windows of a deserted city street, he offered up a silent prayer: "God, if you are there, and if you care, please give me some kind of sign." At that moment, a shabbily dressed man on a bicycle came around the corner riding in the opposite direction. As he passed, he looked the student in the eye and said, "God loves you." Game, set, and match.

I've spoken to a Chinese physicist who converted from atheism to Christianity because ice floats. He told me that every other liquid sinks when it freezes. If water sank when it froze, he assured me, the earth would be entirely lifeless. We exist because water behaves in this odd way. That, he said, cannot be a coincidence and so he believes in our Creator.

I hear stories like these because people feel it's okay to tell a priest things they would find awkward to say in public. Happily, there is a corollary to this instinct: It's okay for a priest to say in public things that would be awkward for other people to say. As a priest, I have a kind of diplomatic immunity from the social taboos against talking about God, or anything else that really matters, in polite company. When I speak up I will at worst see an expression on someone's face that seems to say, "Oh well, what do you expect? He is, after all, a priest." I can speak badly, or I can speak deftly, but at least I'm free to have a go. What I love most about this special priestly license is the freedom it gives me to speak without irony. Almost invariably, when folks do speak about God in public, they hedge their remarks with protective ramparts of irony. That way no one can be certain that they really mean what they say, and if push comes to shove they can pass it all off as a joke. I love not joking. I love being able to speak about God simply and freely from the heart. I love being a priest because, years after the event, people will come up to me and tell me that something I said changed their lives. And more often than not, if I can remember the occasion they are referring to, what they heard is not what I meant to say. I suppose I could be bemused or even annoyed by this; instead I take it as welcome evidence that the Holy Spirit is using me as an instrument through which people hear what God wants them to hear.

Akin to this are occasions when I manage to say something useful during a pastoral encounter that I am dead certain I couldn't have come up with on my own. Again, in those moments, the presence of the Holy Spirit seems palpable. And when I preside at the Eucharist I am the instrument of Christ, who is the real priest. I love being a priest because the Mass is a distillation of what it is to be human. In 1977 two *Voyager* spacecraft were launched carrying golden phonograph records. The records were designed to tell extra-terrestrials what human beings and human culture were like. A great deal of thought was given to what the records should contain. They could have saved a lot of trouble by simply making a recording of the Mass: it's all there. After the Gospel and the Eucharistic Prayer what is there left to say about human nature? And as for culture, the Mass is imbued with cultural riches that reach back through the Middle Ages to ancient Rome and Athens to Mount Sinai and beyond. An epic poem or oratorio could be written about nearly every phrase and gesture. In fact, countless artists, knowingly or not, have taken inspiration from the themes, shape, and textures of the Mass.

For instance, I teach a course about the Catholic novel. For years I have been telling my students that when they have an essay to write for class and are stumped for a topic, there are two questions that can be fruitfully discussed in relation to any Catholic novel. The first is, what is the good news that the novel holds out? No matter how bleakly the human condition may be depicted in a Catholic novel, there will invariably be some element of hope on offer. The second question is whether the main character is ultimately saved. This fundamental theme in Catholic writing goes back at least as far as Everyman and the other morality plays of the fifteenth century. Whether the protagonist lives or dies is a secondary issue. The condition of his or her soul is what really matters. It has occurred to me only recently that these two questions correspond to the two main parts of the Mass. The good news is a kind of gospel. It is analogous to the Liturgy of the Word. The theme of whether the protagonist is saved is ultimately grounded in the Liturgy of the Eucharist in which the Body and Blood of Jesus Christ are offered so that sins may be forgiven.

I was ordained at a time when people were having difficulty saying just what a priest was. Some of us were told we would have to go and find out for ourselves. I found my answers in the parishes where I served. My teachers were devout women who had been members of their local churches for decades. They were spiritual heirs of the prophetess Anna and of the "widows" of New Testament times who practically constituted a distinct office in the Church. In their day these women had seen any number of priests come and go. If anyone knew what a priest was, they did. I set out to benefit from their wisdom. If they were pleased with me I couldn't be going far wrong. I love being a priest because of them.

And I love my order, my particular tribe of priests. I love the Congregation of Holy Cross because when you sit down to dinner in community there will be someone in the room who knows the answer to just about any question you can imagine. I love Holy Cross because in our community there are conversations and arguments that have been going on for thirty years or more. I love Holy Cross because the familiar, unprepossessing fellow sitting next to you is sometimes a world authority in his field, or has poured out his life in selfless service to the people of God, or both. I love Holy Cross because, in a crisis, a fellow with whom you've had an apparently casual, friendly relationship will be revealed as a well of wisdom and compassion. I love that several hundred good men have my back. I love the way we honor each other's fathers and mothers and families. I love that Holy Cross hospitality is legendary. I love that Holy Cross men seem to know instinctively that you do not have to stand on your dignity in order to have dignity. We spend the greater part of our time together talking about sports or the next movie we want to see, but we are having those conversations with men who have given their lives over to service of Christ and his Church with unqualified generosity. They have known success, and had their share of failures, but they are still here, and they are still Christ's men. I love spending time with men who are very different than me in the ways the world cares about, but with whom I am in deep agreement on the things that really matter. I love the high regard we have for good, hard work. I love to sing the Salve Regina with my Holy Cross brothers. I love the way you often discover, after knowing someone for a long time, that they have a profound devotion to the Blessed Virgin Mary. I've found over the years that this turns out to be true of most of the best of us. I love the transformation that seems to come over someone you think you know well, and perhaps have taken for granted, when you have the privilege of seeing him minister to God's people, particularly in a moment of tragedy or great joy. I love the stories about the old days and the great and colorful men who did so much to make us who we are, but who now sleep in Christ. I love that we remember our beloved dead in prayer by name on the anniversary of their deaths. I love that a hundred years after I'm gone someone will be mentioning my name aloud in prayer. I love being able to visit the community cemetery where I will one day be buried myself. I love being able to work in places where we have been so long that the lifeblood of our community is in the bricks. I love to visit a Holy Cross community and its members somewhere in the world for the first time and feel instantly at home. I love the way that members of Holy Cross parishes and schools and universities feel about their priests. I love to visit our seminary and meet young people who remind me of Holy Cross men who have gone before, almost as if there were some kind of spiritually transmitted Holy Cross genetic code. . . .

Father Charlie Gordon, C.S.C., is a professor of theology at the University of Portland. Riveting guy, Charlie: taught in Kenya, earned his doctorate at Cambridge University, has read everything, loves terrible movies.

Perfect Time
A note on the music of being a dad.

CONNOR DOE

FIRST I WAS A GUITAR PLAYER. I was in a band. We were semiprofessionals, meaning that we made a couple of records, and we had publicity photographs, and a MySpace profile, and we got paid sometimes. Then I became a father. Sometimes now I am both a musician and a father but not as much musician as father. Sometimes now I am a father with a guitar and spilled casseroles and crayon scribbles.

Being a guitar player is something like being a father. It works like this: I pick up my guitar or my son and play. If I tickle it just so, it smiles and laughs. I can play the same riff over and over again and it never gets old. If I play something new the guitar doesn't seem to mind but sometimes my son minds. He likes the same thing to be played over and over and over again. In both cases when I play with them they are to a degree extensions of myself. In both cases I remember how to play with them even if I have not played with them for a while.

My son likes music. Maybe all kids do. When he is wild or pouty or whiny I can pick up my guitar and catch his ear. He starts dancing without moving his feet. His face lights up with the purest smile anyone ever saw and he lets whatever it is he is hearing move through him. I think maybe all music is spiritual for kids. Maybe it reminds them of what they are closer to than we are. Maybe it's just sound waves triggering their neurons like tiny pleasant electric shocks. Or maybe it's the presence of something structured and harmonious emanating from outside of themselves that piques their interest and excites them. Whatever the case, my guitar playing makes him happy for as long as just about anything else, except his mom.

Being a father sometimes makes being a guitar player hard, though. Sometimes I am sitting comfortably and minding my own business and strumming my guitar when my son perks up and dances a little and marches over and starts to slap the fretboard with complete joy. Sometimes he palms the strings, muting them. Sometimes he plucks at an open string, creating chordal dissonance. It amuses him to make music in his own way, just like his daddy does.

Another thing I have noticed about playing the guitar while being a dad is that before I was a dad I could pick up my guitar on a whim, dozens of times a day if I wanted to, casually, with plenty of time to play poorly, but now that I am a dad I can only pick it up once or twice a day, and I play it as well as I can. So as a dad I play less and it means more.

Also being a father and a guitar player means that I don't have time any more to fret over incomplete songs, or writer's block, or my missing band. I don't have as much time to spend on me. Maybe that's a great thing. Maybe I had to quit being only a musician in order to truly be the musician I hope to be.

Sometimes I dream about forming a family band with me on guitar, my son on drums, and my wife on bass. She says she would only play the tambourine, which is her way of saying no to being in the band. But still I dream about the family band. I imagine that we begin to practice regularly, and eventually we hit our stride, but then our son hits his teens, and there's that day when playing in a band with his mom and dad is suddenly the most uncool thing ever, and he and his friends form their own band, and things are bittersweet for a while, until his mom and I start a duo with guitar and tambourine.

Once, back when I was just beginning to be a musician and a dad instead of just a musician, my friend Ben and I were playing through some songs a few days before a performance. At one point during our rehearsal, my son, who was pretty new to being a son then, kept perfect time while banging the stick on the floor and grinning jubilantly. I'm not kidding. It didn't last for more than a few beats, and probably it was a complete accident, but it was absolutely perfect. Maybe the best thing about being a dad is that perfect time is always possible.

Connor Doe was a member of Swingin' Amiss, whose song "Passed," from the band's 2005 record Speakeasy, *was on the compact disc included in the Winter 2011 issue of* Portland Magazine.

HEALING OR STEALING?
The Best Commencement Address Ever

PAUL HAWKEN

"You are brilliant, and the earth is hiring. . . ."

WHEN I WAS INVITED to give this speech, I was asked if I could give a simple short talk that was "direct, naked, taut, honest, passionate, lean, shivering, startling, and graceful." Boy, no pressure there.

But let's begin with the startling part. Hey, Class of 2009: you are going to have to figure out what it means to be a human being on earth at a time when every living system is declining, and the rate of decline is accelerating. Kind of a mind-boggling situation—but not one peer-reviewed paper published in the last thirty years can refute that statement. Basically, the earth needs a new operating system, you are the programmers, and we need it within a few decades.

This planet came with a set of operating instructions, but we seem to have misplaced them. Important rules like *don't poison the water, soil, or air,* and *don't let the earth get overcrowded*, and *don't touch the thermostat* have been broken. Buckminster Fuller said that spaceship earth was so ingeniously designed that no one has a clue that we are on one, flying through the universe at a million miles per hour, with no need for seatbelts, lots of room in coach, and really good food—but all that is changing.

There is invisible writing on the back of the diploma you will receive, and in case you didn't bring lemon juice to decode it, I can tell you what it says: YOU ARE BRILLIANT, AND THE EARTH IS HIRING. The earth couldn't afford to send any recruiters or limos to your school. It sent you rain, sunsets, ripe cherries, night-blooming jasmine, and that unbelievably cute person you are dating. Take the hint. And here's the deal: Forget that this task of planet-saving is not possible in the time required. Don't be put off by people who know what is not possible. Do what needs to be done, and check to see if it was impossible only after you are done.

When asked if I am pessimistic or optimistic about the future, my answer is always the same: If you look at the science about what is happening on earth and aren't pessimistic, you don't understand data. But if you meet the people who are working to restore this earth and the lives of the poor, and you aren't optimistic, you haven't got a pulse. What I see everywhere in the world are ordinary people willing to confront despair, power, and incalculable odds in order to restore some semblance of grace, justice, and beauty to this world. The poet Adrienne Rich wrote, "So much has been destroyed I have cast my lot with those who, age after age, perversely, with no extraordinary power, reconstitute the world." There could be no better description. *Humanity is coalescing.* It is reconstituting the world, and the action is taking place in schoolrooms, farms, jungles, villages, campuses, companies, refuge camps, deserts, fisheries, and slums.

You join a multitude of caring people. No one knows how many groups and organizations are working on the most salient issues of our day: climate change, poverty, deforestation, peace, water, hunger, conservation, human rights, and more. This is the largest movement the world has ever seen. Rather than control, it seeks connection. Rather than dominance, it strives to disperse concentrations of power. Like Mercy Corps, it works behind the scenes and gets the job done. Large as it is, no one knows the true size of this movement. It provides hope, support, and meaning to billions of people in the world. Its clout resides in idea, not in force. It is made up of teachers, children, peasants, businesspeople, rappers, organic farmers, nuns, artists, government workers, fisherfolk, engineers, students, incorrigible writers, weeping Muslims, concerned mothers, poets, doctors without borders, grieving Christians, street musicians, the president of the United States of America, and as the writer David James Duncan would say, the Creator, the One who loves us all in such a huge way.

There is a rabbinical teaching that says if the world is ending and the Messiah arrives, first plant a tree, and then see if the story is true. Inspiration is not garnered from the litanies of what may befall us; it resides in humanity's willingness to restore, redress, reform, rebuild, recover, reimagine, and reconsider. "One day you finally knew what you had to do, and began, though the voices around you kept shouting their bad advice," is Mary Oliver's description of moving away from the profane toward a deep sense of connectedness to the living world.

Millions of people are working on behalf of strangers, even if the evening news is usually about the death of strangers. This kindness of strangers has religious, even mythic origins, and very specific eighteenth-century roots. Abolitionists were the first people to create a national and global movement to defend the rights of those they did not know. Until that time, no group had filed a grievance except on behalf of itself. The founders of this movement were largely unknown—Granville Clark, Thomas Clarkson, Josiah Wedgwood—and their goal was ridiculous on the face of it: at that time three out of four people in the world were enslaved. Enslaving each other was what human beings had done for ages. And the abolitionist movement was greeted with incredulity. Conservative spokesmen ridiculed the abolitionists as liberals, progressives, do-gooders, meddlers, and activists. They were told they would ruin the economy and drive England into poverty. But for the first time in history a group of people organized themselves to help people they would never know, from whom they would never receive direct or indirect benefit. And today tens of millions of people do this every day. It is called the world of non-profits, civil society, schools, social entrepreneurship, and non-governmental organizations, of companies that place social and environmental justice at the top of their strategic goals. The scope and scale of this effort is unparalleled in history.

The living world is not "out there" somewhere, but in your heart. What do we know about life? In the words of biologist Janine Benyus, life creates the conditions that are conducive to life. I can think of no better motto for a future economy. We have tens of thousands of abandoned homes without people and tens of thousands of abandoned people without homes. We have failed bankers advising failed regulators on how to save failed assets. Think about this: we are the only species on this planet without full employment. Brilliant. We have an economy that tells us that it is cheaper to destroy earth in real time than to renew, restore, and sustain it. You can print money to bail out a bank but you can't print life to bail out a planet. At present we are stealing the future, selling it in the present, and calling it gross domestic product. We can just as easily have an economy that is based on healing the future instead of stealing it. We can either create assets for the future or take the assets of the future. One is called restoration and the other exploitation. And whenever we exploit the earth we exploit people and cause untold suffering. Working for the earth is not a way to get rich, it is a way to be rich.

The first living cell came into being nearly 40 million centuries ago, and its direct descendants are in all of our bloodstreams. Literally you are breathing molecules this very second that were inhaled by Moses, Mother Teresa, and Bono. We are vastly interconnected. Our fates are inseparable. We are here because the dream of every cell is to become two cells. In each of you are one quadrillion cells, 90 percent of which are not human cells. Your body is a community, and without those other microorganisms you would perish in hours. Each human cell has 400 billion molecules conducting millions of processes between trillions of atoms. The total cellular activity in one human body is staggering: one septillion actions at any one moment, a one with twenty-four zeros after it. In a millisecond, our body has undergone ten times more processes than there are stars in the universe—exactly what Charles Darwin foretold when he said science would discover that each living creature was a "little universe, formed of a host of self-propagating organisms, inconceivably minute and as numerous as the stars of heaven."

So I have two questions for you all: First, can you feel your body? Stop for a moment. Feel your body. One septillion activities going on simultaneously, and your body does this so well you are free to ignore it, and wonder instead when this speech will end. Second question: Who is in charge of your body? Who is managing those molecules? Hopefully not a political party. Life is creating the conditions that are conducive to life inside you, just as in all of nature. What I want you to imagine is that collectively humanity is evincing a deep innate wisdom in coming together to heal the wounds and insults of the past.

Ralph Waldo Emerson once asked what we would do if the stars only came out once every thousand years. No one would sleep that night, of course. The world would become religious overnight. We would be ecstatic, delirious, made rapturous by the glory of God. Instead the stars come out every night, and we watch television.

This extraordinary time when we are globally aware of each other and the multiple dangers that threaten civilization has never happened, not in a thousand years, not in ten thousand years. Each of us is as complex and beautiful as all the stars in the universe. We have done great things and we have gone way off course in terms of honoring creation. You are graduating to the most amazing, challenging, stupefying challenge ever bequested to any generation. The generations before you failed. They didn't stay up all night. They got distracted and lost sight of the fact that life is a miracle every moment of your existence. Nature beckons you to be on her side. You couldn't ask for a better boss. The most unrealistic person in the world is the cynic, not the dreamer. Hope-fulness only makes sense when it is doesn't make sense to be hopeful. This is your century. Take it and run as if your life depends on it.

Paul Hawken is a renowned entrepreneur, visionary environmental activist, and author of many books, among them Blessed Unrest: How the Largest Movement in the World Came into Being and Why No One Saw It Coming.